Crochet
for the
Connoisseur

Crochet for the Connoisseur

Rosemarie Anderson

Photographs by Michael Anderson

B T Batsford London

First published 1979
© Rosemarie Anderson 1979

ISBN 0 7134 1144 9

Filmset in 'Monophoto' Optima by
Servis Filmsetting Limited, Manchester
Printed in Great Britain by
The Anchor Press Ltd, Tiptree, Essex
for the publishers B T Batsford Limited
4 Fitzhardinge Street, London W1H 0AH

Contents

All yarns mentioned in this book are available at time of printing. For any queries regarding yarns do not hesitate to phone or write to the spinners, listed on page 119. Should any of the yarns mentioned become unavailable, the chapter on Tension (pages 82 to 85) will enable you to work with an equivalent yarn

Acknowledgment

My grateful thanks to all those who helped to make this book possible. In particular to my husband Michael, the photographer. To the models, my friends May, Pauline and Mioko and to Carol Allcinder, who is just embarking on a modelling career and to whom I wish every future success. My thanks also to Virginia, who helped in times of pressure; Alex Graham at the Battersea Arts Centre and Tony Newell of The Victoria, East Sheen for permitting us to use his beergarden. Not forgetting, of course, Shirley McLaughlin whose initial idea it was to change my hobby into a career.

¶ntroduction

I have prepared this book for the *connoisseur* of crochet, not only for the person who knows how to crochet, but also for those who know a few basic stitches and want to learn more.

I am self-taught, so in many ways am as much a beginner as some of my readers and I have advanced only through years of constant practice and trial and error.

The attraction of these patterns is their extreme simplicity. All have been specially prepared for this book and will not be found elsewhere. Although some of the garments may not appear so on first sight, they are *all* easy to make. Some might take a little patience because the stitch is monotonous, but in the end it is the very simplicity of the stitch that makes the garment special. So, do have patience, the end will justify the effort.

The yarns chosen may not always be the cheapest on the market (unfortunately, wool has risen in cost in line with everything else) however, most of the designs, especially the evening coat, work out very reasonably indeed.

Do not economise on the cost of yarn, see the saving in the fact that you are *making* the garment. The wrong yarn for the right garment can have a negative effect on the respect felt for the garment and ultimately, of course, on the wearing of it.

Finally, if you are dissatisfied with your present way of using a crochet hook and are willing to try a new approach, carefully study the techniques shown in the last section of the book, also the hints, many of which experience has taught me and which I have found useful. I wish you many happy hours of relaxation.

Rosemarie Anderson

London 1979

Patterns

Day suit

See colour section between pages 48 and 49

Materials   *Top*   2(3:3:3) balls of *Pingouin Pescadou* M
3(3:3:4) balls of *Pingouin Pescadou* C
crochet hook no. 3.00
Skirt   10(10:11:11) balls of *Pingouin Pescadou* M
2(3:3:4) balls of *Pingouin Pescadou* C
waist measure of appropriately coloured petersham
18cm. (7in.) zip fastener

Measurement   to fit bust 81(86:91:96)cm
32(34:36:38)in.
Top   Length from under arm 27cm (10¼in.)
Skirt   Length 70cm (27½in.) (adjustable)

Tension   10st(s) and 5 rows to 5cm (2in.)

Abbreviations/explanations   page 119

Top

Front

With C make 80(86:92:98) ch

Foundation row   1 tr into 4th ch from hook;
1 tr into each of next ch to end; 78(84:90:96) st(s);
turn.

Block pattern

Note   When changing colour, finish preceding
tr in the new colour (ie last 2 loops on hook).
Leave yarn attached and carry it along at the base
of row when not in use, working over it in the new
colour. Beginning row with 3ch (for 1st tr) miss st
under hook.
* *1st row*   * M – 6 tr; C-6 tr repeat from * 5(6:6:7)
times; M – 6(0:6:0) tr, working last tr into 3rd ch;
turn.
Note   Twist M(C:M:C) once round C(M:C:M) to
bring up to next working level.

2nd row   M(C:M:C) – 0(6:0:6) tr; * C(M:C:M) –
6 tr; M(C:M:C) – 6 tr repeat from * 5(6:6:7) times;
C(M:C:M) – 6(0:6:0) tr; turn.
Work 4 more rows of tr, always working 2-row M
blocks over C and 2-row C blocks over M. Now
work 6 more rows of tr in 2-row stripe sequence
C,M,C*.
Repeat from * 1st row to * 12th row.

Shape armhole

Next row   C – ss over next 7 st(s); 3 ch (to count
as 1st tr); 1 tr into each of next 5 tr; continue in
block pattern to within last 6 st(s); turn.
Work 5 more rows in block pattern.

Shape neck

Next row   continue in block pattern over next
18 st(s); turn.
Work 13(14:15:16) rows in block pattern. Fasten off.
Complete second side to match first.

Back

Instructions as for front, but start off block pattern
with M(C:M:C) to give an uninterrupted block
pattern all the way round.

To make up

Join side and shoulder seams. Now work 2 rounds
of dc, evenly spaced, round neck and armhole
edges.

Skirt

Adjustment in length should be done before the
start of the border. To shorten adjust on rounds
worked between increasing rounds. To lengthen
add appropriate number of rounds before the
start of the border.

With M make 122(132:142:152) ch for waist edge.

Foundation row   1 tr into 4th ch from hook; 1 tr
into each of next ch to end; 120(130:140:150)
st(s); turn.

Tr row   3 ch (to count as 1st tr) miss st under
hook; 1 tr into each of next tr to end, working last
tr into 3rd ch; turn.

1st inc row   3 ch (to count as 1st tr) miss st under
hook; 1 tr into each of next 4(5:5:6) tr; 2 tr into
next tr; * 1 tr into each of next 11(12:13:14) tr; 2 tr
into next tr; repeat from * 8 times; 1 tr into each
of remaining tr, working last tr into 3rd ch;
130(140:150:160) st(s); turn.

Work 15 more rows of tr, inc 10 st(s) on every 3rd
row (ie on next inc row work 2 tr in every
13th(14th:15th:16th) tr, on next inc row in every
14th(15th:16th:17th) tr and so on, bearing in mind
that on the very 1st inc of every inc row only half

Figure 1 showing petersham waistband and wrong side of zip

the number of st(s) (or as near to half as possible) are worked at the beginning of the row and the remainder at the end), last inc row 180(190:200: 210) st(s). Join last row with a ss into 1st tr (ie 3rd ch) to form a ring. Continue working in rounds always turning at the end.

Work 29 more rounds of tr, inc 10 st(s) as before on every 3rd round, last inc round 270(280:290: 300) st(s).

Next inc round increase 6(8:10:12) tr, evenly spaced, over this round to bring the number of st(s) to 276(288:300:312); turn.

Border

* Work 6 more rounds of tr in 2-row stripe sequence C,M,C,*.

Block pattern

(See note for block pattern top front)

1st round * M – 6 tr (counting 3 ch at the beginning as 1st tr); C – 6 tr; repeat from * to end; turn.

Bring the yarn that is not in use up to next working level.

Repeat previous row once.

3rd round * C – 6 tr; M – 6 tr; repeat from * to end; turn.

Repeat previous round once.

Repeat 1st and 2nd round once.

Repeat from * to * of border. Fasten off.

To make up

With M work 1 round of dc, evenly spaced, all round waist edge and side opening. Sew zip fastener in place and join petersham to waist edge. *Note* Zip should be worn at the side. To avoid bulging round sitting area wear garment back to front occasionally.

Figure 2   shows closed zip right side

Bikini beach outfit

Materials 3(4:5) balls of *Twilleys Goldfingering* crochet hooks nos 2.00 and 3.00

Measurements to fit bust 81(86:91)cm 32(34:36)in.
straps 41cm (16in.)

Tension 14 dc and 16 rows of dc to 5cm (2in.) worked on hook no 3.00

Abbreviations/explanations page 119

Top
Cup (make 2)

With hook no 3.00 make 41(45:49) ch.

1st row 1 dc into 2nd ch from hook; 1 dc into each of next ch to end; 40(44:48) st(s); turn.

Dc row 1 ch; 1 dc into each of next dc; turn. Work 12(14:16) more rows of dc.

Next row 1 ch; 1 dc into each of next 20(22:24) dc; turn.
Repeat previous row 19(21:23) times more. Fasten off.
Join side seam to make into cup. Make 2nd cup.

With right side of work facing rejoin hook no 2.00 in 1st of foundation ch (side seam on the right) and work 1 dc into each of next ch to end; join to 2nd cup (side seam on the left) by working 1 dc into each of next foundation ch to end; turn. Work 2 more rows of dc.
Now work 1 row of dc, evenly spaced, around remaining edges.

Straps (make 4) length adjustable

With hook no 3.00 make 121 ch.

1st row 1 dc into 2nd ch from hook; 1 dc into each of next ch; turn.

2nd row ss into each of next dc to end. Fasten off.

To make up

Sew straps in position and tie in bows.

Pants

Note these are meant to be very brief, adjust as necessary.

Front

With hook no 3.00 make 15(16:17) ch.

1st row 1 dc into 2nd ch from hook; 1 dc into each of next ch to end; 14(15:16) st(s); turn.
Work 10(11:12) more rows of dc; always turning with 1 ch.

Inc row 1 ch; 1 dc into 1st dc; 2 dc into next dc; 1 dc into each of next dc to within last 2 dc; 2 dc into next dc; 1 dc into last dc; 2 st(s) inc; turn.
Work 1 row of dc.
Repeat previous 2 rows alternately 14(15:16) times last row 44(47:50) st(s); turn.
Repeat inc row 6(8:10) times; last row 56(63:70) st(s). Fasten off.

Back

With wrong side of work facing rejoin yarn in crotch in 1st of foundation ch and work 10(11:12) rows of dc.
Repeat inc row 26(27:28) times; last row 66(69:72) st(s).
Now work 24(28:32) more rows of dc, inc 1 st at each end on every 2nd row; last row 90(97:104) st(s). Do not fasten off.

Edgings/loops

Change to hook no 2.00 and work 1st loop thus: * work 3 dc down side edge (ie work 1 dc to each row); 4 ch; turn; ss into 1st dc; turn; 6 dc into loop; now continue with dc, evenly spaced, all the way along side edge to top row; work 2nd loop thus: – 4 ch; turn; ss into 3rd dc from end; turn; 6 dc into ring; ss into 2nd dc of top row; continue with ss along top edge; repeat from *. Fasten off.

Tie straps (make 2)

Work as for bikini top straps. Thread through loops and tie in bows.

Sun suit

Materials   5(6:6) balls of *Twilleys Goldfingering* M
1(1:1) ball of *Twilleys Goldfingering* C
crochet hook no 3.00

Measurements   to fit bust 81(86:91)cm
32(34:36)in.

Tension   14 dc and 16 rows of dc to 5cm (2in.)
14 tr and 7 rows of tr to 5cm (2in.)

Abbreviations/explanations   *page 119*

Front

With M make 4 ch.

1st row   4 tr into 4th ch from hook; turn.

2nd row   3 ch, to count as 1st tr; 2 tr into 1st tr
(ie st under hook); tr into each of next 3 tr; 3 tr
into last tr (ie 3rd ch); 9 st(s); turn.

3rd row   3 ch, to count as 1st tr; 2 tr into 1st tr;
tr into each of next tr to within last st; 3 tr into
last st (ie 3rd ch); 4 st(s) inc; turn.
Repeat previous row 24(26:28) times more; last
row 109(117:125) st(s). Change to C.
Repeat previous row 5 times more in colour
sequence: C,C,M,M,C; last row 129(137:145) st(s).

Shape sides

Next row   continue in C; 3 ch (these do not
count as 1 tr); work 1st, 2nd and 3rd tr together;
tr into each of next tr to within last 3 st(s); work 3
tr together (inserting hook into last 2 tr and 3rd
ch); 125(133:141) st(s); turn.

Next row   Change to M; 3 ch (these do not count
as 1 tr); work 1st, 2nd and 3rd tr together; tr into
each of next tr to within last 3 st(s); work 3 tr
together; 4 st(s) dec; turn.
Repeat previous row in colour sequence M,C,C,M
– to end, until 5 st(s) remain; work 5 tr together.
Do not fasten off.
Continue with M and work 70(73:76) dc, evenly
spaced, all along top edge. Fasten off.
Work similar edge along lower edge. Fasten off.

Crotch/back

1st row   With right side of work facing rejoin M in
18th st from end and work 1 dc into each of next
36(39:42) dc; turn.

2nd row   1 ch; 1 dc into 1st dc; work 2 dc

together; 1 dc into each of next dc to within last
3 st(s); work 2 dc together; 1 dc into last dc; 2
st(s) dec; turn.
Repeat previous row 9(11:12) times; last row
14(15:16) st(s).
Now work 21(23:25) rows of dc, always working 1
turning ch at the end of each row.
Work 38(41:44) rows of dc, inc 1 dc in 2nd st from
end and beginning of each row; last row 90(97:
104) st(s).

Shape back

Next row   1 ch; 1 dc into each of next 8(10:12) dc;
work 2 dc together; turn.

Next row   1 ch; work 1st and 2nd dc together;
1 dc into each of next dc to end; turn.

Next row   1 ch; work 1st and 2nd dc together;
1 dc into each of next dc to end; turn.
Repeat previous 2 rows alternately all st(s) are dec.
Fasten off.
Complete second side to match first, reverse all
shaping.

To make up

Work 1 row of dc, evenly spaced, along both sides
of front and back. Join back to front. Work 1
round of dc, evenly spaced, round each leg.
Fasten off. With right side of work facing work 1
row of dc, evenly spaced, all along back edge
starting from under arm.

Next row   4 ch; miss 1st dc; 1 tr into next dc;
* 1 ch; miss 1 dc; 1 tr into next dc; repeat from *
to end; turn.

Next row   1 ch; 1 dc into each of next tr and ch
sp to end.
Now work 1 row of dc along Front top edge.
Fasten off.

Ties (make 2)

Make 2 ch; 1 dc into 2nd ch; * 1 dc into previous
dc; repeat from * until ties measure 86cm (34in.).
Now work 1 row of dc all along side of ties. Fasten
off.

Sew ties in position. Thread each tie through 1st
ch sp (under arm); criss-cross and thread through
15th ch sp (or whichever required). Tie in a bow.

Flower motif shawl

Materials   11 balls of *Pingouin Confortable* crochet hooks nos 4.00 and 4.50

Measurements   Length 242cm (95in.)   Depth 132cm (52in.)

Abbreviations/explanations   *page 119*

With hook no 4.50 make 6 ch.

1st row   1 tr each into 5th and 6th ch from hook; turn.

2nd row   4 ch (to count as 1 tr); 2 tr into 1st tr (ie st immediately under hook); miss 1 tr; 1 ch; 3 tr – called 1 cluster into next tr (ie 4th·ch); turn.

3rd row   4 ch; 2 tr into 1st tr; 1 ch; 1 cluster into next ch sp; 1 cluster into last st; turn.

4th row   4 ch; 2 tr into 1st tr; 1 ch/1 cluster into each of next 2 ch sp(s); 1 ch; 1 cluster into last st; turn.

5th row   5 ch; 1 tr into 1st tr; * 1 ch; miss 1 tr; tr into next tr; 1 ch; miss ch sp; 1 tr into next tr; * repeat from * to * twice; ending 1 ch/1 tr into 1 ch/1 tr into last st; turn.

6th row   4 ch; 2 tr into 1st tr; * 1 ch; miss ch sp; tr into next tr *; repeat from * to * to within 5 ch sp; 1 ch; 1 cluster into 4th of 5 ch; turn.

7th row   4 ch; 2 tr into 1st tr; 1 ch; 1 cluster into next ch sp; repeat from * to * 6th row 6 times; 1 ch; miss next ch sp; 1 cluster into next ch sp; 1 ch; 1 cluster into last st; turn.

8th row   4 ch; 2 tr into 1st tr; 1 ch/1 cluster into each of next 2 ch sp(s); repeat from * to * 6th row 4 times; 1 ch/1 cluster into each of next 2 ch sp(s); 1 ch; 1 cluster into last st; turn.

9th row 4 ch; 2 tr into 1st tr; 1 ch/1 cluster into each of next 3 ch sp(s); repeat from * to * 6th row twice; 1 ch/1 cluster into each of next 3 ch sp(s); 1 ch; 1 cluster into last st; turn.

10th row   5 ch; 1 tr into 1st tr; repeat from * to * 5th row 4 times; work 1 tr/1 ch into each of next 2 tr (missing ch in between); repeat from * to * 5th row 3 times; 1 ch; miss 1 tr; into last st work 1 tr 1 ch/1 tr; turn.

11th row   4 ch; 2 tr into 1st tr; ** repeat from * to * 6th row 8 times; 1 ch; miss 1 ch sp; 1 cluster into next ch sp **; repeat from ** to ** to end,

working last cluster into 4th of 5 ch; turn.

12th row   4 ch; 2 tr into 1st tr; 1 ch; 1 cluster into next ch sp; ** repeat from * to * 6th row 6 times; miss 1 ch sp; 1 ch/1 cluster into each of next 2 ch sp(s)**; repeat from ** to ** to end, working last cluster into last st; turn.

13th row   4 ch; 2 tr into 1st tr; 1 ch/1 cluster into each of next 2 ch sp(s); ** repeat from * to * 6th row 4 times; miss next ch sp; 1 ch/1 cluster into each of next 3 ch sp(s); ** rep from ** to ** to end, working last cluster into last st; turn.

14th row   4 ch; 2 tr into 1st tr; 1 ch/1 cluster into each of next 3 ch sp(s); ** repeat from * to * 6th row twice; miss next ch sp; 1 ch/1 cluster into each of next 4 ch sp(s) **; repeat from ** to ** to end, working last cluster into 4th ch; turn.

15th row   5 ch; 1 tr into 1st tr; * 1 ch; miss next st (ch sp to count as 1st); tr into next tr *; repeat from * to * to including 1st tr of last cluster; 1 ch; into 4th of 5 ch work 1 tr/1 ch/1 tr; turn.

Repeat row 11 to 15 fourteen times. Do not fasten off.

Border

Change to hook no 4.00 and work down side as follows:

Next row   6 ch; tr into top of 1st tr; 3 ch; tr into the base of next tr; * 3 ch; 1 tr into the base of next tr; repeat from * all along side edge to within base of last tr at centre point; into centre st work 3 ch/1 tr/3 ch/1 tr/3 ch/1 tr – 1 ch sp group made –; repeat from * all along side edge to within last tr; 3 ch; into last tr work 1 tr/3 ch/1 tr; turn.

Next row   6 ch; 1 tr into 1st tr; * 3 ch; miss ch sp; 1 tr into next tr; repeat from * to including 1st tr of ch sp group: into centre tr of ch sp group work 3 ch/1 tr/3 ch/1 tr/3 ch/1 tr; repeat from * to including last tr; 3 ch, into 3rd of 6 ch work 1 tr/3 ch/1 tr; turn.
Repeat previous row 4 times more.

Picot edging

Continue working along top row.
* 3 ch; 1 dc into 1st of 3 ch; 1 dc into next sp; repeat from *, evenly spaced, all along top row, Fasten off.

Flower motif (make 19)

With hook no 4.50 make 6 ch; ss into 1st ch to form a ring.

1st round   6 ch; 1 tr into ring; ★ 3 ch; 1 tr into ring; repeat from ★ 3 times; 3 ch, ss into 3rd of 6 ch.

2nd round   ★ into next ch sp work 1 dc/1 htr/3 tr/ 1 htr/1 dc; repeat from ★ into each of next 5 ch sp(s); ss into 1st dc.

3rd round   ★ 5 ch; pass these ch behind the petal of the previous round, ss into the back of next tr of 1st round; repeat from ★ 5 times, working last ss into the 1st ch at the beginning of round.

4th round   into each of next 6 ch sp(s) work 1 dc/1 htr/5 tr/1 htr/1 dc; ss into 1st dc. Fasten off. Sew motifs, evenly spaced, to border.

Fringed shawl

Materials 7 balls of *Pingouin Poudreuse*
crochet hook no 6.00

Measurements Length 194cm (76¼in.) Depth
100cm (39½in.)

Tension 7 tr to 5cm (2in.) 8 rows of tr to 11.50cm
(4½in.)

Abbreviations/explanations *page 119*

Note for chevron pattern see pages 86 and 87.
Make 6 ch.

1st row 2 tr into 4th ch from hook; 3 tr into each of next 2 ch; – 9 st(s); turn.

2nd row 3 ch (to count as 1st tr); 2 tr into 1st tr (ie st immediately under hook); tr into each of next 3 tr; 5 tr – called 1 cluster – into next tr; tr into each of next 3 tr; 3 tr into last tr; – 17 st(s); turn.

3rd row 3 ch (to count as 1st tr); tr into each of next tr to including 2nd tr of cluster; 1 cluster into next tr (ie centre tr of cluster); tr into each of next tr to within last tr; 3 tr into 3rd ch; – 8 st(s) inc; turn. Repeat previous row 33 times more; last row 289 st(s).

Lacy border

Next row ∗ 5 ch; miss 2 tr; 1 dc into next tr; repeat from ∗ to including 2nd tr of cluster; 5 ch; miss next tr; 1 dc into next tr; repeat from ∗ to within 3rd tr from end; miss 1 tr; tr into 3rd ch; turn.

Next row 5 ch; 1 dc into 1st ch sp; ∗ 5 ch; 1 dc into next ch sp; into next dc work 3 tr; 1 dc into next ch sp; into next dc work 3 tr; 1 dc into next ch sp; repeat from ∗ 15 times, ending with last dc into sp above cluster of last tr row; working 5 ch and next dc into same sp repeat from ∗ 16 times; 5 ch; 1 dc into next ch sp; 3 ch; 1 tr into 1st ch of 5 ch; turn.

Next row 5 ch; 1 dc into 1st ch sp; ∗ 5 ch; 1 dc into next ch sp; 5 ch; 1 dc into centre tr of tr group; into next dc work 2 tr/1 dtr/2 tr; 1 dc into centre tr of next tr group; repeat from ∗ to including centre tr of last tr group; 5 ch; 1 dc into next ch sp; 5 ch; 1 dc into last tr; turn.

Next row ∗ 5 ch/1 dc into each of next ch sp(s); 5 ch/1 dc into dtr ∗; repeat from ∗ to ∗ to including last dtr; 5 ch/1 dc into each of next ch sp(s); 1 tr into 1st of 5 ch; turn.
Do not fasten off, but work 1 row of dc, evenly spaced, all along upper edge.
Fasten off.

Fringe

Instructions pages 115–117.
Take six 46cm (18in.) lengths of yarn.

gacket with zip front

Materials 7(8:8:9) balls of *Pingouin Poudreuse* M
1(1:1:1) ball of *Pingouin Poudreuse* C
crochet hook no 4.00
1 heavy open-end zip fastener

Measurements to fit bust 81(86:91:96)cm
32(34:36:38)in.
Length from under arm (adjustable) 44.5cm
(17½in.)
Sleeve length from under arm 46cm (18in.)

Tension 9 tr and 4 rows to 5cm (2in.)
Abbreviations/explanations page 119

Yoke

With M make 76(82:88:94) ch for neck edge.

Inc row tr into 4th ch from hook; 1 tr into each
of next 11(12:13:14) ch; 3 tr into next ch; 1 tr into
each of next 9(10:11:12) ch; 3 tr into next ch; 1 tr
into each of next 26(28:30:32) ch; 3 tr into next
ch; 1 tr into each of next 9(10:11:12) ch; 3 tr into
next ch; 1 tr into each of next 13(14:15:16) ch; –
82(88:94:100) st(s); turn.

Next inc row 3 ch (to count as 1st tr), miss st
under hook (throughout pattern); * 1 tr into each
of next tr to including 1st tr of 3 tr cluster; 3 tr into
next tr (ie centre tr of cluster); repeat from * 3
times; 1 tr into each of next tr to end, work last tr
into 3rd ch (throughout pattern); – 8 st(s) inc;
turn. Repeat previous row 15(16:17:18) times; last
row 210(224:238:252) st(s).

Division for sleeves

Next row 3 ch (to count as 1st tr); tr to including
centre tr of tr cluster; * 4(5:6:7) ch; miss all st(s) to
including 1st tr of next cluster; * 1 tr into each of
next tr to including 1st tr of next cluster; repeat
from * to * once; 1 tr into each of next tr to end;
turn.
Next row 3 ch (to count as 1st tr); 1 tr into each
of next tr and ch to end; 132(142:152:162) st(s);
turn.

Next row 3 ch (to count as 1st tr); inc 3(2:1:0) tr
on this row to bring number of st(s) to
135(144:153:162); turn.

Inc row 3 ch (to count as 1st tr); 1 tr into each of
next 6(6:7:7) tr; 2 tr into next tr; * 1 tr into each of

next 14(15:16:17) tr; 2 tr into next tr; repeat from *
7 times; 1 tr into each of remaining 7(7:8:9) tr; –
144 (153:162:171) st(s); turn. Work 25 more rows,
inc 9 st(s) on every 5th row (ie on next inc row
work 2 tr into every 16th(17th:18th:19th) tr, on the
next inc row in every 17th(18th:19th:20th) tr and
and so on; bearing in mind that on the very 1st
inc of every inc row only half the number of st(s)
(or as near to half as possible) is worked at the beginning of the row and the remainder at the end;
last row 189(198:207:216) st(s).
Work 7 more rows of tr.

First sleeve

Work in rounds

1st round With wrong side of work facing rejoin
M in centre st under arm; 3 ch (to count as 1st tr);
1 tr into each of next 1(2:2:3) tr; 2 tr over next tr;
tr into centre tr of cluster; 1 tr into each of next tr
to including centre tr of next cluster; 2 tr over
next tr; 1 tr into each of next 2(2:3:3) tr; ss into
3rd ch; 53(57:61:65) st(s); turn.

Tr round 3 ch (to count as 1st tr); 1 tr into each
of next tr to end; ss into 3rd ch; turn.

Work 35 more rounds of tr. Fasten off.

Second sleeve

Work as for first sleeve to including 2nd round.
Now work in stripe sequence: C – 3 rows; M – 2
rows; C – 3 rows; M – 27 rows. Fasten off.

Draw strings

Take 3 strands each 102cm (40in.) long for sleeve
draw strings and 3 strands 234.5cm (36in.) long for
hip draw string and follow instructions, page 118.
Thread the first two draw strings through last
sleeve row and the third, longer draw string
through lower hip edge.

Collar

1st row With right side of work facing rejoin M in
corner st of neck row and work 1 dc into each of
next tr to end; turn.

2nd row 1 ch; 1 dc into each of next dc to end;
turn.
Work 18 more rows of dc. Do not fasten off, but
work 1 row of dc, evenly spaced, all the way down
front edge. Fasten off and work the same edge up
other side. Fasten off.

To make up

Join in zip fastener to halfway up collar. Fold remaining half of collar inwards and stitch down along zip and all along neck edge.

Ꝺardigan with border contrast

Materials
7(8:8:9) balls of *Pingouin Pescadou* M
1(1:1:1) ball of *Pingouin Pescadou* C
crochet hooks no 3.00 and 3.50

Measurements
to fit bust 81(86:91:96)cm
32(34:36:38)in.
Length from under arm (excluding border)
40(41:42:43)cm   15¾(16¼:16½:16¾)in.

Tension
22 st(s) to 10cm (4in.) and 11 rows of tr
to 10cm (4in.) worked on hook no 3.00

Abbreviations/explanations   page 119

With hook no 3.00 and M make 65(71:77:83) ch
for neck edge.

1st row   2 tr into 4th ch from hook; 1 tr into each
of next 14(16:18:20) ch; 3 tr into next ch – called
1 cluster; 1 tr into each of next 30(32:34:36) ch;
1 cluster into next ch; 1 tr into each of next
14(16:18:20) ch; 3 tr into last ch; – 70(76:82:88)
st(s); turn.

2nd row   3 ch (to count as 1st tr); 1 tr into 1st tr
(ie st immediately under hook); 1 cluster into next
tr; ★ 1 tr into each of next tr to including 1st tr of
cluster; 1 cluster into next tr (ie centre tr of cluster
repeat from ★ twice; 2 tr into last st (ie 3rd ch);
80(86:92:98) st(s); turn.

3rd row   3 ch (to count as 1st tr); 1 tr into 1st tr;
★ 1 tr into each of next tr to including 1st tr of
cluster; 1 cluster into next tr (ie centre tr of
cluster); repeat from ★ 3 times; 1 tr into each of
next tr to within last st; 2 tr into last tr (ie 3rd ch);
10 st(s) inc.
Turn.

Repeat previous row 16(17:18:19) times; last row
250(266:282:298) st(s).

Divide for arm holes

Next row   3 ch (to count as 1st tr) miss st under
hook; ★ 1 tr into each of next tr to including centre
tr of next cluster; 1(3:5:7) ch; miss all st(s) to
including 1st tr of next cluster; repeat from ★ once;
1 tr into each of next tr to end, working last tr into
3rd ch (throughout pattern); turn.

Next row   3 ch (to count as 1st tr, throughout
remaining pattern) miss st under hook; 1 tr into
each of next tr and ch to end; – 148(160:172:184)
st(s); turn.

Next row   3 ch, miss st under hook; 1 tr into each
of next tr to end; turn.
Repeat previous row 33(34:35:36) times more.

1st sh row   3 ch, miss st under hook; work next
2 tr together; 1 tr into each of next tr to within
last 3 tr; work last 3 tr together; turn.

2nd sh row   3 ch (these do not count as 1 tr);
work 1st, 2nd and 3rd tr together; 1 tr into each of
next tr to within last 3 tr; work 3 tr together – 4
st(s) dec; turn.
Repeat previous row 3 times more.

Sleeves

With wrong side of work facing and hook no 3.00
rejoin M under arm in centre st. Continue work in
rounds.

1st round   3 ch (to count as 1st tr); work 2(3:4:5)
tr to within 2nd tr of cluster of previous row; 1 tr
into each of next tr to including 2nd tr of next
cluster of previous row; work 2(3:4:5) tr, evenly
spaced, to end; ss into 3rd ch; – 59(65:71:77) st(s);
turn.

2nd round   3 ch (to count as 1st tr); 1 tr into each
of next 3 tr; work 2 tr together; 1 tr into each of
next tr to within last 5 tr; work 2 tr together; 1 tr
into each of next 3 tr; ss into 3rd ch; 57(63:69:75)
st(s) turn.
Repeat previous round twice; last round
53(59:65:71) st(s); turn.
Work 11 more rounds of tr.

Sleeve border

Work 4 more rounds of dc in colour sequence
M,C,C,M, always turning at the end of each round
with 2 ch (to count as 1st dc). Fasten off.
With hook no 3.50 rejoin M in centre st of back
neck edge and work the same border as for
sleeves. Fasten off.

Sun top summer dress

Material 11(12:12) balls of *Pingouin Pescadou* M
1(1:1) ball of *Pingouin Pescadou* C
crochet hook no 3.00
One zip fastener 18cm (7in.) long

Measurements to fit bust 81(86:91)cm
32(34:36)in.
Length from under arm 90cm (35½in.)

Tension 22st(s) and 9½ rows to 10cm (read
comments on tension, page 82).

Abbreviations/explanations page 119

Note This simple dress is worked almost entirely
in tr, from the top downwards with adjustable
length. The zip on the side makes it possible to
wear the dress back to front occasionally. This
helps prevent a bulge around the sitting area.

With M make 145(156:167) ch.

Foundation row 1 tr into 4th ch from hook; 1 tr
into each of next ch to end; – 143(154:165) st(s);
turn.

Tr row 3 ch (to count as 1st tr), miss st under
hook; 1 tr into each of next tr to end, work last tr
into 3rd ch; turn.
Work 14 more tr rows, joining last row with a ss
into 1st tr (ie 3rd ch); turn.
Now work in rounds.

Next round 3 ch (to count as 1st tr); 1 tr into
each of next tr to end of round; ss into 3rd ch;
turn.
Work 8(9:10) more rounds of tr.

1st Inc round 3 ch (to count as 1st tr); 1 tr into
each of next 5 tr; 2 tr into next tr; * 1 tr into each
of next 12(13:14) tr; 2 tr into next tr; repeat from *
9 times; 1 tr into each of remaining tr to end; ss
into 3rd ch; (11 st(s) inc); – 154(165:176) st(s).

Work 58 more rounds of tr, inc 11 st(s) twice on
every 3rd round, then on every 4th round (ie on
the next inc round work 2 tr into every
14th(15th:16th) tr; on the next inc round 2 tr in
every 15th(16th:17th) tr and so on; bearing in mind
that on the very first inc of every inc round half
the number, or as near to half as possible, is
worked at the beginning of the round and the
remainder at the end); last round 308(319:330)
st(s).

Lower edge

Work 4 more rounds of dc in colour sequence
M,C,C,M; always turning with 2 ch.
Fasten off.
Work the same edge along top edge, ending with
1 row of dc, evenly spaced, along side opening.
Fasten off.

Straps (make 2) length adjustable

With M make 66 ch.

1st row 1 dc into 2nd ch from hook; 1 dc into
each of next ch to end; – 65 st(s); turn.
Work 3 more rows of dc in colour sequence
C,C,M.

Next row M – ss into each of next dc to end.
Fasten off.

To make up

Sew straps in place and fit in zip. Straps and top
edge can be supported with petersham edging, if
necessary.

Evening dress

Materials 17(19:21) balls of *Twilley's Goldfingering* M
2(2:2) balls of *Twilley's Goldfingering* C
crochet hooks no 2.50 and 3.00
Two 51cm (20in.) lengths of petersham ribbon
6mm ($\frac{1}{4}$in.) wide
2 fancy buttons
One 15cm (6in.) zip fastener.

Measurements to fit bust 81(86:91)cm
32(34:36)in.
Length from waist: (adjustable) 76cm (30in.)

Tension 14 st(s) and 7 rows of tr to 5cm (2in.)

Abbreviations/explanations page 119

Note The top for this dress is worked in two triangular shaped parts, which allow for stretch. The skirt is added after completing the upper part.

Top

1st Triangle (make two)

With hook no 3.00 and M make 4 ch.

1st row into 4th ch from hook work 2 tr; turn.

2nd row 3 ch, (to count as 1st tr); 2 tr into 1st tr (ie st immediately under hook); 1 tr into each of next 2 tr, working last tr into 3rd ch; – 5 st(s); turn.

3rd row 3 ch (to count as 1st tr), miss st under hook; 1 tr into each of next tr to within last tr; 3 tr into last tr (ie 3rd ch); – 2 st(s) inc; turn.

4th row 3 ch (to count as 1st tr); 2 tr into 1st tr; 1 tr into each of next tr to end, working last tr into 3rd ch; – 2 st(s) inc; turn.
Repeat previous 2 rows alternately 31(34:37) times; last row 71(77:83) st(s). Fasten off.

Border

1st row With hook no 2.50 rejoin M in corner st of 1st row and work 65(70:75) dc, evenly spaced all along widest edge of triangle; now work 5 dc into corner st; continue with dc into each of next tr down front edge; 1 ch; turn.

2nd row With C work 1 dc into each of next dc to including 2nd dc of cluster; 5 dc – called 1 cluster – into next dc (ie centre dc); 1 dc into each of next dc to within last dc; 2 dc into last dc; turn.

3rd row 1 ch; 2 dc into 1st dc; 1 dc into each of next dc to including 2nd dc of cluster; 1 cluster into next dc; 1 dc into each of next dc to end; turn. Repeat 2nd and 3rd row once in M and once in C. Fasten off.

Skirt

Lay out both triangles to form one large triangle (apex pointing towards you). With hook no 3.00 rejoin M in corner st of right triangle and work 65(72:78) dc, evenly spaced, along borderless edge; now continue on 2nd triangle with a further 65(71:78) dc; – 130(143:156) st(s); turn.

1st row 3 ch (to count as 1st tr), miss st immediately under hook (throughout pattern); 1 tr into each of next dc to end; turn.

2nd row 3 ch (to count as 1st tr); 1 tr into each of next 5 tr; 3 tr into next tr; * 1 tr into each of next 12 tr; 3 tr into next tr; repeat from * 8(9:10) times; 1 tr into each of next 6 tr; – 150(165:180) st(s); turn.

3rd row 3 ch; work 3 tr together; 1 tr into each of next 4 tr; 3 tr into next tr; * 1 tr into each of next 6 tr; miss 2 tr; 1 tr into each of next 6 tr; 3 tr

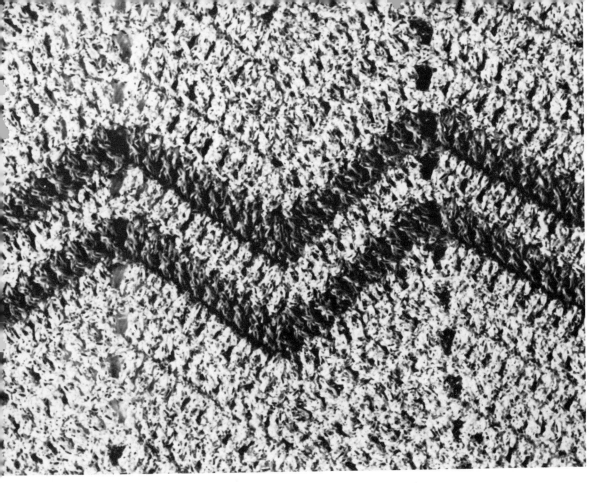

into next tr; repeat from * 8(9:10) times; 1 tr into each of next 4 tr; work next 2 tr together; tr into last tr (ie 3rd ch); turn.

4th row   3 ch; work 2 tr together; 1 tr into each of next tr to within centre tr of cluster; * 3 tr into centre tr of cluster; 1 tr into each of next tr to tr before sp; miss next 2 tr; 1 tr into each of next tr to within centre tr of cluster; repeat from * 8(9:10) times; 1 tr into each of next tr to within 3rd tr from end; work 2 tr together; 1 tr into last st (ie 3rd ch); turn.

Inc row   3 ch; work 2 tr together; 1 tr into each of next tr to within centre tr of cluster; * 5 tr into centre tr of cluster; 1 tr into each of next tr to within tr before sp; miss next 2 tr; 1 tr into each of next tr to within centre tr of cluster; repeat from * 8(9:10) times; 1 tr into each of next tr to within 3rd tr from end; work 2 tr together; tr into last st (ie 3rd ch); – 170(187:204) st(s); turn.
Repeat 4th row twice.
Work 1 inc row.
Repeat 4th row 3 times.
With C work 1 inc row; – 190(209:228) st(s).
With M repeat 4th row once.

With C repeat 4th row once.
Continue in M and repeat 4th row twice.
Work 1 inc row; – 210(231:252) st(s).
Repeat 4th row once and join with a ss into 1st tr; ss into next tr; turn.
Now work in rounds.

Tr round   3 ch; miss 2 tr; 1 tr into each of next tr to within centre tr of cluster; * 3 tr into centre tr of cluster; 1 tr into each of next tr to within tr before sp; miss 2 tr; 1 tr into each of next tr to within centre tr of cluster; repeat from * 8(9:10) times; 1 tr into each of next tr to end; ss into 3rd ch; ss through next 2 tr; turn.
Work 65 more rounds, inc next on 5th round; then 5 times on every 11th round; last 3 rounds to end in C;M;C. Fasten off.

To make up

With M work one row of dc, evenly spaced, round zip opening. Join in zip fastener. Sew straps (petersham ribbon) in place and tie in a bow at the back. Attach buttons to triangle tips to strengthen straps.

See colour section between pages 48 and 49

Summer dress with bow tie front

Materials   11(12:13) balls of *Pingouin Pescadou*
crochet hooks no 2.50 and 3.00
75cm (29½in.) polyester satin
2 buttons

Measurements   to fit bust 81(86:91)cm
32(34:36)in.
Length from under arm (adjustable)
87(88.5:89.5)cm 34¼(34¾:35¼)in.

Tension   worked on hook no 3.00 11 tr to 5cm
(2in.) and 5 rows of tr to 5cm (2in.)

Abbreviations/explanations   page 119

Yoke

With hook no 3.00 make 53(59:65) ch for neck
edge.

1st row   1 tr into 4th ch from hook; 1 tr into each
of next 10(12:14) ch; 3 tr into next ch – called 1
cluster –; 1 tr into each of next 26(28:30) ch; 1
cluster into next ch; 1 tr into each of next 10(12:14)
ch; 2 tr into last ch; – 56(62:68) st(s); turn.

2nd row   3 ch (to count as 1st tr); 1 tr into 1st tr;
★ 1 tr into each of next tr to including 1st tr of
cluster; 1 cluster into next tr (ie centre tr of cluster);
repeat from ★ once more; 1 tr into each of next tr
to within last st; 2 tr into 1st tr (ie 3rd ch); –
62(68:74) st(s); turn.
Repeat previous row 19(20:21) times more; last
row 176(188:200) st(s).

Divide for armholes and join front and back

Now work in rounds.

Next round   make 4(6:8) ch; miss all tr to
including 1st tr of next cluster; 1 tr into next tr (ie
centre tr of cluster); 1 tr into each of next tr to
including 1st tr of next cluster; 1 tr into next tr (ie
centre tr of cluster); make 1(3:5) ch; miss all tr to
last st; 1st tr into last st (ie 3rd ch); make 68(72:76)
ch; ss into 3rd of first 4(6:8) ch at beginning of
round; ss through next 1(2:3) ch. Turn.

Next round   3 ch (to count as 1st tr); 1 tr into each
of next 0(1:2) ch; 1 tr into next tr; 1 tr into each of
next 68(72:76) ch; 1 tr into next tr; 1 tr into each of
next 1(3:5) ch; 1 tr into each of next tr to end; 1 tr

into each of next 0(1:2) ch; ss into 3rd ch; –
142(154:166) st(s); turn.

Next round   3 ch (to count as 1st tr); 1 tr into
each of next tr to end; ss into 3rd ch; turn.
Repeat previous round 23(24:25) times more.

Next round   bring this round up to 143(154:165)
st(s) by inc (–:dec) 1 tr anywhere on this round; ss
into 3rd ch; turn.

1st Inc round   3 ch (to count as 1st tr); 1 tr into
each of next 5 tr; 2 tr into next tr; ★ 1 tr into each
of next 12(13:14) tr; 2 tr into next tr; repeat from ★
9 times; 1 tr into each of remaining tr; ss into 3rd
ch; 11 st(s) inc; – 154(165:176) st(s); turn.
Work 53(54:55) more rounds of tr, inc 11 st(s) on
every 4th round (ie on next inc round work 2 tr in
every 14th(15th:16th) st, on next inc round in every
15th (16th:17th) st and so on). Bearing in mind that
on the 1st inc half (or as near to half as possible)
the number of st(s) of the inc is worked at the
beginning of the round and the remainder at the
end. Last round 297(308:319) st(s). Fasten off.

Sleeve borders

With hook no 2.50 and right side of work facing,
rejoin yarn under arm and work 59(65:71) dc
round sleeve edge, ss into 1st dc; turn.
Work 3 more rounds of dc. Fasten off.

Neck border

With hook no 2.50 and right side of work facing,
rejoin yarn at centre back neck edge; 1 dc into
each ch to corner; 4 ch for corner loop; miss next
row end; now work 38(40:42) dc, evenly spaced,
down side of neck; 1 dc into each of next tr along
front neck edge; 38(40:42) dc, evenly spaced, up
other side of neck, missing last row end; 4 ch for
corner loop; 1 dc into each of next ch along back
neck edge to centre; ss into 1st dc; turn.
Work 1 more round of dc; work 4 dc into each
corner loop; fasten off.

To make up

Join front neck and front sleeve edges together
over approximately 4cm (1½in.) along from sleeve
edge. Sew buttons to the ends of polyester satin,
then thread through corner loops. Tie in a bow.

Summer top with peplum

Materials 5(6:7) balls of *Twilley's Goldfingering* M
1(1:1) ball of *Twilley's Goldfingering* C
crochet hook no 3.00

Measurements small (medium:large)

Tension 14 tr to 5cm (2in.) 11 rows of tr to
7.5cm (3in.)

Abbreviations/explanations page 119

Note For chevron pattern see pages 86 and 87.

Panel (make 4)

With M make 6 ch.

1st row 2 tr into 4th ch from hook; 3 tr into each
of next 2 ch; turn.

2nd row 3 ch (to count as 1st tr); 2 tr into 1st tr
(ie st immediately under hook); 1 tr into each of
next 3 tr; 5 tr – called 1 cluster – into next tr; 1 tr
into each of next 3 tr; 3 tr into last tr (ie 3rd ch);
17 st(s); turn.

3rd row 3 ch (to count as 1st tr); 1 tr into each of
next tr to including 2nd tr of cluster; 1 cluster into
next tr (ie centre tr of cluster); 1 tr into each of
next tr to within last st; 3 tr into 3rd of 3 ch; – 8
st(s) inc; turn.
Repeat previous row 4(5:6) times more; last row
57(65:73) st(s).

Shape sides

Next row 3 ch (these do not count as 1 tr); work
1st, 2nd and 3rd tr together; tr into each of next tr
to including 2nd tr of cluster; 1 cluster into next
tr; 1 tr into each of next tr to within last 3 st(s);
work 3 tr together; turn.

Repeat previous row 10(11:12) times; then twice in
C and twice in M; noting that the number of st(s)
does not alter, as the 4 tr which are inc when
working the cluster are dec at the beginning and
end of each row. Fasten off.

To make up

Join 4 panels, 2 panels forming the front and 2
forming the back.

Peplum

Work in rounds.

1st round rejoin M in either seam st and work
130(143:156) dc along waist edge.

Note To divide st(s) equally over the round, work
quarter of the number of st(s) to each panel; ss
into 1st dc; turn.

2nd round 3 ch (to count as 1st tr); tr into each
of next 5 tr; 3 tr into next tr; ★ 1 tr into each of
next 12 tr; 3 tr into next tr; repeat from ★ 8(9:10)
times; 1 tr into each of remaining 6 tr; ss into 3rd
ch; ss into next tr; – 150(165:180) st(s); turn.

3rd round 3 ch (to count as 1st tr); miss 2 tr; 1 tr
into each of next tr to including 1st tr of 3 tr
cluster; ★ 3 tr into next tr (ie centre tr of 3 tr
cluster); 1 tr into each of next tr to within last tr
before sp; miss 2 tr; 1 tr into each of next tr to
including 1st tr of 3 tr cluster; repeat from ★
8(9:10) times; 1 tr into each of remaining tr; ss into
3rd ch and next tr; turn.

Repeat previous round once.

Inc round work as for 3rd round, but work 5 tr
instead of 3 tr for each cluster; – 170(187:204)
st(s); turn.
★ Repeat 3rd round twice. Work 1 inc round. ★
Repeat from ★ to ★ once.
Repeat 3rd round 6 times more, work in stripe
sequence M,C,M. Fasten off.

Straps (adjustable)

Make 61 ch (or as many as required).

1st row htr into 2nd ch from hook; htr into each
of next ch to end; turn.

2nd row ss along side of last st; 1 ch; now work 1
htr into the base of each of next htr to end. Fasten
off. Sew in place.

Ribbon-threaded summer top

Materials   3(4:4) balls of *Pingouin Pescadou* M
1(2:2) ball(s) of *Pingouin Pescadou* C
crochet hook no 3.00
one 127cm (50in.) length and two 60cm (23½in.)
lengths of polyester satin 6mm (¼in.)

Measurements   to fit bust 81(86:91)cm 32(34:36)in.
Length from under arm (excluding border):
30.50(31.50:32.50)cm; 12(12½:12¾)in.

Tension 11 tr to 5cm (2in.) 5 rows of tr to 5cm (2in.)

Abbreviations/explanations   page 119

Note   For chevron pattern see pages 86 and 87.

Front/back (both alike)

With M (C:M) make 2 ch.

1st row   into 2nd ch from hook work 5 dc; turn.

2nd row   1 ch; 2 dc into 1st dc; 1 dc into next dc;
3 dc into next dc; 1 dc into next dc; 2 dc into last
dc; – 9 dc; turn.
Continue in 2-row stripe sequence, leaving
threads attached.

3rd row   C (M:C); 1 ch; 2 dc into 1st dc; 1 dc into
each of next dc to including 1st of 3 dc; 3 dc into
next dc (ie centre dc); 1 dc into each of next dc to
within last dc; – 4 st(s) inc; turn.
Repeat previous row 17(19:21) times more, remaining in 2-row stripe sequence; last row 81(89:97)
st(s). Fasten off C, continue with M to end.

Next row   3 ch (to count as 1st tr); 2 tr into 1st dc;
1 tr into each of next dc to including 1st of 3 dc;
5 tr – called 1 cluster – into next dc; 1 tr into each
of next dc to within last dc; 3 tr into last dc;
89(97:105) st(s); turn.

Next row   3 ch (to count as 1st tr); 2 tr into 1st tr;
1 tr into each of next tr to including 2nd tr of
cluster; 1 cluster into next tr (ie centre tr of cluster);
1 tr into each of next tr to within last tr; 3 tr into
last tr (ie 3rd ch); – 8 st(s) inc; turn.
Repeat previous row twice; last row 113(121:129)
st(s).

Shape sides

Next row   3 ch, miss 1st tr; work next 2 tr together;
continue in pattern to within last 3 st(s); work 3 tr
together (insert hook into each of last 2 tr and 3rd
ch); turn.

Next row   3 ch (these do not count as 1 tr); work
1st 3 tr together; continue in pattern to within last
3 st(s); work 3 tr together; turn.
Repeat previous row 7 times more, noting that the
number of st(s) does not alter, as the 4 tr that are
inc when working the cluster, are dec at the
beginning and end of each row.

Next row   repeat previous row to within tr before
cluster; work 3 tr together (ie next tr and 1st and
2nd tr of cluster); – 52(56:60) st(s); turn.

Next row   3 ch (these do not count as 1 tr); work
3 tr together; 1 tr into each of next tr to within
last 3 st(s); work 3 tr together; – 4 st(s) dec; turn.
Repeat previous row until 4 st(s) remain.

Next row   3 ch; miss 1st tr; work 3 tr together.
Fasten off.
With wrong side of work facing rejoin yarn in 4th
tr of cluster and complete 2nd side to match the
1st, reversing all shaping.

Top cuff

Work in rounds.

1st round   Rejoin C in back centre st; 2 ch (to
count as 1st dc); now work 20(22:24) dc, evenly
spaced, to including last C chevron row; 44(48:52)
ch; continue with 42(46:50) dc, evenly spaced,
along dc edge of front chevron; 44(48:52) ch;
continue with 21(23:25) dc, evenly spaced, along
the remainder of dc edge to end; ss into 1st dc;
turn.

2nd round   2 ch (to count as 1st dc); 1 dc into
each of next dc and ch to end of round; ss into
1st dc; – 172(188:204) st(s); turn.

3rd round   4 ch; miss next dc; * tr into next dc;
1 ch; miss next dc * ; repeat from * to * to end of
round; ss into 3rd of 4 ch; turn.

4th round   2 ch (to count as 1st dc); 1 dc into
each of next ch sp and tr to end; turn.
Work 1 more round of dc. Fasten off.

To make up

Work an even number of dc, evenly spaced, all
along lower edge.
Repeat 3rd and 4th round as for top cuff. Fasten
off.
Thread 2 ribbons through cuff edge. Tie in bows.
Repeat on lower edge with 1 ribbon.

ℒacy edged summer top

Materials   6(7:8:9) balls of *Twilley's Crysette* crochet hook no 3.00

Measurements   to fit bust 81(86:91:96)cm 32(34:36:38)in.
Length from under arm (excluding peplum) 24(25:26:27)cm 9½(9¾:10¼:10¾)in.

Tension   8 ch sp(s) to 5cm (2in.)   11 rows of ch sp(s) to 10cm (4in.)

Abbreviations/explanations   page 119

Bodice

Make 64(68:72:76) ch.

Foundation row   1 tr into 6th ch from hook; * 1 ch; miss 1 ch; tr into next ch; repeat from * to end; 30(32:34:36) ch sp(s) made; turn.

Pattern row   4 ch; miss 1st ch sp; tr into next tr; * 1 ch; miss next ch sp; tr into next tr; repeat from * to end, work last tr into 3rd of 4 ch; turn. Repeat previous row 88(94:100:106) times more. Do not fasten off.

Edges

Repeat pattern row all along upper and lower edge at a medium tension; – 90(96:102:108) ch sp(s). Join seam.

Lacy border

Make 25 ch.

1st row   tr into 6th ch from hook; * 1 ch; miss 1 ch; tr into next ch; repeat from * to within last ch; 1 tr into last ch; turn.

2nd row   3 ch (to count as 1 tr); miss st under hook; tr into next tr; * 1 ch; miss ch sp; tr into next tr; * repeat from * to * to end, work last tr into ch sp; turn.

3rd row   4 ch; miss 1st ch sp; tr into next tr; repeat from * to * 2nd row to within last tr; tr into 3rd ch; turn.

4th row   6 ch; tr into 1st tr; tr into next tr; * miss ch sp; 1 ch; Pc st into next tr; 1 ch; miss ch sp; tr into next tr; repeat from * 4 times; work last tr into 3rd of 4 ch; turn.

5th row   4 ch; miss 1st ch sp; tr into Pc st; 1 ch/ 1 tr into each of next tr and Pc st to within last tr, missing ch sp(s) in between; tr into last tr; 13 tr into 6 ch sp; miss 1st tr of previous row and ss up 3 ch of the next row; turn.

6th row   3 ch; 1 dc into 1st of 3 ch (1 picot made); miss 1st of 13 tr; tr into next tr; * make 1 picot; miss next tr; tr into next tr; repeat from * 5 times; tr into next tr; repeat from * to * 2nd row to end, working last tr into 3rd of 4 ch; turn.

7th row   Repeat 3rd row to within last tr; tr into last tr; turn.

Repeat row 2 to 7 13(14:15:16) times.
Repeat row 2 to 6 once.

Do not fasten off, but work pattern row all along straight edge; – 90(96:102:108) ch sp(s) made.

Note   the number of ch sp(s) should be equal to the number of ch sp(s) along upper and lower bodice edge.

Join each border to form a ring. With right side of work facing, join 1st border to lower edge to form peplum. Join 2nd border to upper edge by working 1 dc into each of next ch sp and tr, insert hook through both layers of work; ss into 1st dc; turn.

Next round   4 ch; miss 1 dc; 1 tr into next dc; 1 ch; * miss 1 dc; tr into next dc; 1 ch; repeat from * to end; ss into 3rd of 4 ch. Fasten off.

Straps (make 2)

Make 6 ch.

1st row   1 htr into 2nd ch from hook; 1 htr into each of next ch to end; turn.

2nd row   1 ch; 1 htr into each of next htr to end; turn. Repeat previous row until strap measures 55cm (21½in.) or required length. Sew straps in place.

Make a draw string with 6 strands of yarn as described on page 118. Thread through waist row and tie in a bow.

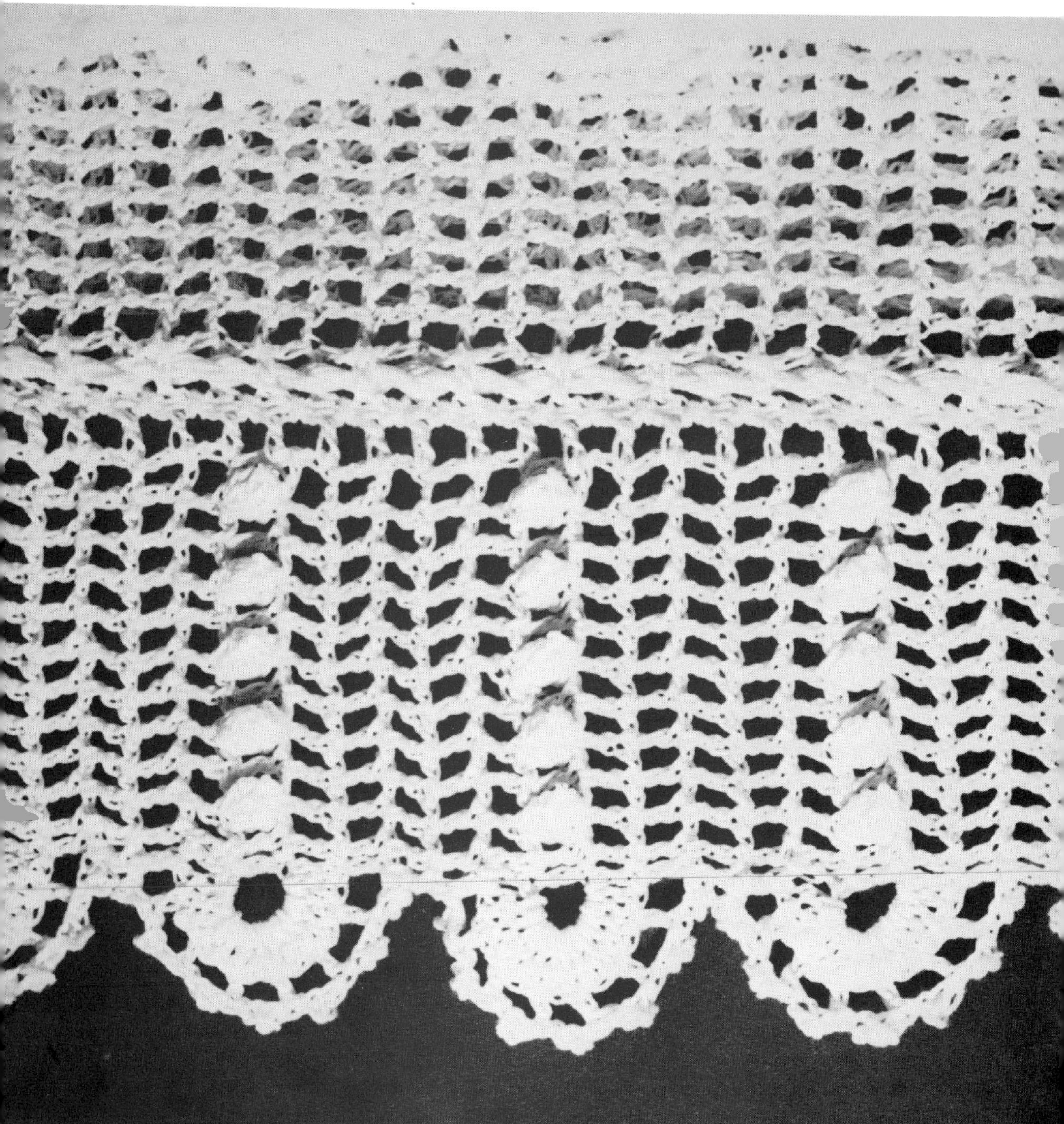

Mandarin style day coat

Materials
13(14:15:16) balls of *Pingouin Podium*
crochet hook no 4.00
9m (10yd) braid
8 small toggle hooks matching colour of braid
four medium sized toggle hooks to hold side vents
together, again matching the colour of the braid

Measurements
to fit bust 81(86:91:96cm)
32(34:36:38)in.
Length from under arm (adjustable) 82.5cm
(32½in.)
Sleeve Length from under arm (adjustable)
44.5cm (17½in.)

Tension
9 tr and 4 rows to 5cm (2in.)

Abbreviations/explanations *page 119*

Yoke

Make 68(74:80:86) ch for neck edge.

Foundation row 1 tr into 4th ch from hook; 1 tr
into each of next ch to end; 66(72:78:84) st(s);
turn.

Inc row 3 ch (to count as 1st tr) miss st under
hook; 1 tr into each of next 11(12:13:14) tr; 3 tr –
called 1 cluster – into next tr; 1 tr into each of
next 7(8:9:10) tr; 1 cluster into next tr; 1 tr
into each of next 24(26:28:30) tr; 1 cluster into
next tr; 1 tr into each of next 7(8:9:10) tr; 1 cluster
into next tr; 1 tr into each of next tr to end,
working last tr into 3rd ch; – 74(80:86:92) st(s);turn.

Next inc row 3 ch (to count as 1st tr) miss st under
hook (throughout pattern); * 1 tr into each of next
tr to including 1st tr of cluster; 1 cluster into next
tr (ie centre tr of cluster); repeat from * 3 times; 1
tr into each of remaining tr to end, working last tr
into 3rd ch (throughout pattern); – 82(88:94:100)
st(s); turn.
Repeat previous row 14(15:16:17) times, last row
194(208:222:236) st(s).

Division for sleeves

Next row 3 ch; * 1 tr into each of next tr to
including centre tr of next cluster: 4(5:6:7) ch;
miss all st(s) to including 1st tr of next cluster;
repeat from * once; 1 tr into each of next tr to
end; turn.

Next row 3 ch; 1 tr into each of next tr and ch to

end; – 124(134:144:154) st(s); turn.

Tr row 3 ch; 1 tr into each of next tr to end;
turn.
Work 2 more rows of tr.

Front panel

Next row 3 ch; 1 tr into each of next 29(32:35:38)
st(s); turn.

Sh row 3 ch; 1 tr into each of next 2 tr; inc 1 tr
by working 2 tr into next tr; 1 tr into each of next
tr to end; turn.
Work 60 more rows of tr, inc 1 tr in 4th tr from
end/beginning (alternately) of every 3rd row.
Fasten off.
Miss 64(68:72:76) central st(s) at the back. With
wrong side of work facing rejoin yarn in 30th
(33rd:36th:39th) tr from end with 3 ch (to count as
1st tr) and complete 2nd panel to match 1st,
reversing all shaping. Fasten off.

Back panel

Miss 2 tr under arm and with wrong side of work
facing rejoin yarn to back row.

1st row 3 ch; 1 tr into each of next 59(63:67:71)
tr; turn.

Sh row 3 ch; 1 tr into each of next 2 tr; inc 1 tr
by work 2 tr into next tr; 1 tr into each of next tr
to within 4th st from end; inc 1 tr by working 2 tr
into next tr; 1 tr into each of remaining 3 tr; turn.
Work 60 more rows of tr, inc 1 tr in 4th tr from
beginning and end of every 3rd row. Fasten off.

Sleeves (length adjustable)

Work in rounds.

Tr round rejoin yarn in centre st under arm; 3
ch (to count as 1st tr); work 5(6:7:8) tr, evenly
spaced, to including centre tr of cluster; 1 tr into
each of next tr to within centre tr of next cluster;
work 5(6:7:8) tr, evenly spaced, to end of round,
ss into 3rd ch; – 50(55:60:65) st(s); turn.

Dec round 3 ch (to count as 1st tr); 1 tr into each
of next 3(4:5:6) tr; work 2 tr together; 1 tr into
each of next tr to within 5th(6th:7th:8th) tr from
end; work 2 tr together; 1 tr into each of remaining tr; ss into 3rd ch; 48(53:58:63) st(s); turn.
Work 1 more dec round; 46(51:56:61) st(s); turn.
Work 9 more rounds of tr.

Inc round   inc 4 tr, evenly spaced, over this round; turn.
Work 23 more rounds of tr, inc 4 tr, evenly spaced, on every 3rd round. Fasten off.

Collar

With right side of work facing, rejoin yarn in corner st of neck edge and work 1 dc into each foundation ch; 66(72:78:84) dc.
Work 11 more rows of dc.
Fold collar in half towards inside and stitch down in position.

Edgings

Rejoin yarn in front top corner st and work 1 row of dc, evenly spaced, around all edges (ie front, lower, vent, back lower, 2nd vent, 2nd lower front and front edges), ending at top corner of collar. Fasten off.

To make up

Join braid to all edges, with double edge around collar. Sew two medium-sized toggle hooks to vents. Join small toggle hooks, evenly spaced, to front edges, last toggle hook to be in line with lower side toggle.

Evening outfit with harem trousers

Materials   *Top*   23(24:25) balls of *Twilley's Goldfingering*
Harem trousers   12(13:14) balls of *Twilley's Goldfingering*
crochet hook no 3.00
one waist and two ankle measures of elastic

Measurements   to fit bust 81(86:91)cm 32(34:36)in.
Top   length from neck edge to tip (measures without tassels)   57cm (22½in); *drop*: 5cm (2in.)
Trousers   inside leg 75cm (29½in.), adjustable

Tension   8 ch sp(s) and 6 rows to 5cm (2in.)

Abbreviations/explanations   page 119

Top
Front/Back (both alike)

Make 5 ch.

1st row   into 5th ch from hook work tr/1 ch/tr/1 ch/tr/1 ch/tr; turn.

2nd row   4 ch; tr into 1st tr; * 1 ch; tr into next tr *; 1 ch; into next tr work tr/1 ch/tr/1 ch/tr – one cluster made; repeat from * to * once; 1 ch; into 3rd of 4 ch work tr/1 ch/tr; turn.

3rd row   4 ch; tr into 1st tr; repeat from * to * of previous row to including 1st tr of cluster; 1 ch work 1 cluster into next tr (ie centre tr of cluster); 1 ch; repeat from * to * of previous row to last tr; 1 ch; into 3rd of 4 ch work tr/1 ch/tr; – 12 ch sp(s); turn.

Repeat previous row 17(18:19) times; last row 80(84:88) ch sp(s).

1st shaping row   3 ch; miss 1st tr; 1 tr into next tr; continue in pattern to within 1st ch sp; work 2 tr together (insert hook into last tr and 3rd of 4 ch); turn.

2nd shaping row   3 ch; miss 1st tr; tr into next tr; continue in pattern to within 2nd tr from end; work 2 tr together (insert hook into each of next 2 tr); turn.
Repeat previous row once.

* *Inc row*   3 ch; miss 1st tr; tr into next tr; 1 ch; into next tr work 1 tr/1 ch/1 tr; continue in pattern to within 4th tr from end; into 4th tr work 1 tr/1 ch/1 tr; 1 ch; tr into next tr; 1 ch; work last 2 tr together; turn.
Repeat 2nd shaping row 3 times. *
Repeat from * to * 7 times. Fasten off.

To make up

Join side seams. Rejoin yarn under arm in side seam st and work 162(170:178) dc, evenly spaced, all long top edge; ss into 1st dc. Work 1 more round of dc.

Next round   5 ch; miss 2 dc; * 1 tr into next dc; 2 ch; miss 2 dc *; repeat from * to * to end; ss into 3rd ch; turn.

Next round   1 ch; 2 dc into ch sp; * 1 dc into next tr; 2 dc into ch sp; repeat from * to end; ss into 1st ch. Fasten off.

Straps (length adjustable)

Rejoin yarn in 7th tr from under arm of front neck edge and work 73 ch; ss into 7th tr from under arm of back neck edge; ss into each of next 3 st(s); miss 1st strap ch; * 1 tr into next ch; miss next ch; repeat from * to end; 1 ch; ss into 8th tr of front neck edge. Fasten off.
Work 2nd strap.
Now work 1 round of dc around strap, front and back neck edges. Fasten off.

Tassels

Instructions pages 115–117, *see* Fringe.
Each strand measures 23cm (9in.). Use 2 strands for each tassel.
To cut a number of strands at once, wind each ball of yarn (one at a time) round a longish piece of cardboard, measuring 11.5cm (4½in.) in height
Now cut along one edge. Begin in 12th row from the bottom and work upwards. * Work 1 tassel into each ch sp over next 5 rows (fill in one extra tassel where necessary). Now miss 7 rows. *

See colour section between pages 72 and 73

Repeat from * to * 3 times.

Note To stop tassels from loosening it helps to have a bowl of water at hand. After the tassel is made, wet the knot a little, pull once more tightly. Allow to dry.

Harem trousers (length adjustable)

Make 176(192:208) ch for waist edge; ss into 1st ch to form a ring.

1st round 4 ch; miss 1st ch; * 1 tr into next ch; 1 ch; miss 1 ch; repeat from * to end; ss into 3rd of 4 ch; – 88(96:104) ch sp(s); turn.

2nd round 4 ch; miss 1st ch sp; * 1 tr into next tr; 1 ch; miss next ch sp; repeat from * to end; ss into 3rd of 4 ch; turn.
Work 4 more rounds of ch sp(s).

1st inc round 4 ch; miss 1st ch sp; * 1 tr into next tr; 1 ch; miss next ch sp *; repeat from * to * 4(4:5) times; ** into next tr work 1 tr/1 ch/1 tr; 1 ch; miss next ch sp; repeat from * to * 10(11:12) times **; repeat from ** to ** 6 times; into next tr work 1 tr/1 ch/1 tr; 1 ch; miss next ch sp; repeat from * to * to end; ss into 3rd of 4 ch; – 96(104: 112) ch sp(s); turn.
Work 6 more rounds of ch sp(s).

2nd inc round 4 ch; miss 1st ch sp; * 1 tr into next tr; 1 ch; miss next ch sp *; repeat from * to * 4(5:5) times; ** into next tr work 1 tr/1 ch/1 tr; 1 ch; miss next ch sp; repeat from * to * 11(12:13) times **; repeat from ** to ** 6 times; into next tr work 1 tr/1 ch/1 tr; 1 ch; miss next ch sp; repeat from * to * to end; ss into 3rd of 4 ch; – 104(112:120) ch sp(s); turn.
Work 6 more rounds of ch sp(s).

3rd inc round 4 ch; miss 1st ch sp; * 1 tr into next tr; 1 ch; miss next ch sp *; repeat from * to * 5(5:6) times; ** into next tr work 1 tr/1 ch/1 tr; 1 ch; miss next ch sp; repeat from * to * 12(13:14) times **; repeat from ** to ** 6 times; into next tr work 1 tr/1 ch/1 tr; 1 ch; miss next ch sp; repeat from * to * to end; – 112(120:

128) ch sp(s); turn.
Work 3 more rounds of ch sp(s).

4th inc round 4 ch; miss 1st ch sp; * 1 tr into next tr; 1 ch; miss next ch sp *; repeat from * to * 5(6:6) times; ** into next tr work 1 tr/1 ch/1 tr; 1 ch; miss next ch sp; repeat from * to * 13(14:15) times **; repeat from ** to ** 6 times; into next tr work 1 tr/1 ch/1 tr; 1 ch; miss next ch sp; repeat from * to * to end; ss into 3rd of 4 ch; – 120(128: 136) ch sp(s); turn.
Work 3 more rounds of ch sp(s).

5th inc round 4 ch; miss 1st ch sp; * 1 tr into next tr; 1 ch; miss next ch sp *; repeat from * to * 6(6:7) times; ** into next tr work 1 tr/1 ch/1 tr; 1 ch; miss next ch sp; repeat from * to * 14(15:16) times **; repeat from ** to ** 6 times; into next tr work 1 tr/1 ch/1 tr; 1 ch; miss next ch sp; repeat from * to * to end; ss into 3rd of 4 ch; – 128(136:144) ch sp(s); turn.
Work 2 more rounds of ch sp(s).

Divide for crotch

Make 15(19:23) ch; ss into 65th(69th:73rd) tr (counting the 3 ch immediately below as 1st tr); 1 ch. Fasten off.

1st Leg

1st round: With wrong side of work facing rejoin yarn in 8th(10th:12th) of the 15(19:23) ch; 4 ch; miss 1 ch; * 1 tr into next ch; 1 ch; miss 1 ch; repeat from * 2(3:4) times; 1 ch; continue with ch sp(s) to within 1st of crotch ch; miss 1st ch; repeat from * to end; ss into 3rd of 4 ch; – 74(78:82) ch sp(s); turn.
Work 93 more rounds of ch sp(s) or as many as required. Fasten off.

To make up

Thread elastic through waist edge and bottom leg row.

47

Full-length evening coat

Materials   23(25:27) balls of *Pingouin Poudreuse*
crochet hook no 4.00
one fancy hook and eye

Measurements   to fit bust 81(86:91)cm
32(34:36)in.
Length from under arm   99cm (39in.)   *Drop* 10cm
(4in.)
Sleeve length from under arm   42cm (16½in.)
Drop   5cm (2in.)

Tension   5 ch sp(s) to 5cm (2in.) and 9 pattern
rows to 10cm (4in.)

Abbreviations/explanations   *page 119*

Yoke

Make 84(96:108) ch for neck edge.

1st row   1 tr into 6th ch from hook; * 1 ch; miss
1 ch; 1 tr into next ch *; repeat from * 5(6:7) times;
** 1 ch; miss 1 ch; into next ch work 1 tr/1 ch/1 tr/
1 ch/1 tr – called 1 cluster; repeat from * to *
3(4:5) times; repeat from ** to ** once; repeat
from * to * 15(17:19) times; repeat from ** to **
once; repeat from * to * 3(4:5) times; repeat from
** to ** once; repeat from * to * to end; –
48(54:60) ch sp(s); turn.

2nd row   4 ch; miss 1st ch sp; 1 tr into next tr;
* 1 ch; miss next ch sp; 1 tr into next tr *; **
repeat from * to * to including 1st tr of cluster **;
*** 1 ch; miss next ch sp; 1 cluster into next tr (ie
centre tr of cluster) ***; repeat from * to * and
** to ** and *** to *** 3 times; repeat from * to
* to end; 8 ch sp(s) inc; turn.
Repeat previous row 11(12:13) times; last row
152(166:180) ch sp(s).

Divide for armholes

Next row   4 ch; miss 1st ch sp; 1 tr into next tr; *
continue in ch sp(s) to including centre tr of next
cluster; miss all st(s) to including 1st tr of next
cluster; 1 ch; miss next ch sp; repeat from * once;
continue in ch sp(s) to end; 88(96:104) ch sp(s);
turn.

Next row   4 ch; miss 1st ch sp; 1 tr into next tr;
continue in ch sp(s) to end, gaining 1 ch sp each
under armhole; 90(98:106) ch sp(s); turn.
Work 13 more rows of ch sp(s).

1st inc row   4 ch; miss 1st ch sp; 1 tr into next tr;
work 3(2:1) more ch sp(s); 1 ch; miss next ch sp;
into next tr work 1 tr/1 ch/1 tr; * work 9 more ch
sp(s); 1 ch miss next ch sp; into next tr work 1 tr/
1 ch/1 tr; repeat from * 7(8:9) times; continue with
ch sp(s) to end; – 99(108:117) ch sp(s); turn.
Work 14 more rows of ch sp(s).

2nd inc row   4 ch; miss 1st ch sp; 1 tr into next tr;
work 4(4:5) more ch sp(s); 1 ch; miss next ch sp;
into next tr work 1 tr/1 ch/1 tr; * work 10(11:12)
more ch sp(s); 1 ch; miss next ch sp; into next tr
work 1 tr/1 ch/1 tr; repeat from * 7 times; continue
with ch sp(s) to end; – 108(117:126) ch sp(s); turn.
Work 10 more rows of ch sp(s).

3rd inc row   4 ch; miss 1st ch sp; 1 tr into next tr;
work 4(5:5) more ch sp(s); 1 ch; miss next ch sp;
into next tr work 1 tr/1 ch/1 tr; * work 11(12:13)
more ch sp(s); 1 ch; miss next ch sp; into next tr
work 1 tr/1 ch/1 tr; repeat from * 7 times; continue
with ch sp(s) to end; 117(126:135) ch sp(s); turn.
Work 10 more rows of ch sp(s).

4th inc row   4 ch; miss 1st ch sp; 1 tr into next tr;
work 5(5:6) more ch sp(s); 1 ch; miss next ch sp;
into next tr work 1 tr/1 ch/1 tr; * work 12(13:14)
more ch sp(s); 1 ch; miss next ch sp; into next
tr work 1 tr/1 ch/1 tr; repeat from * 7 times;
continue with ch sp(s) to end; – 126(135:144) ch
sp(s); turn.
Work 10 more rows of ch sp(s).

5th inc row   4 ch; miss next ch sp; 1 tr into next
tr; work 5(6:6) more ch sp(s); 1 ch; miss next ch sp;
into next tr work 1 tr/1 ch/1 tr; * work 13(14:15)
more ch sp(s); 1 ch; miss next ch sp; into next tr
work 1 tr/1 ch/1 tr; repeat from * 7 times; continue with ch sp(s) to end; – 135(144:153) ch sp(s);
turn.
Work 6 more rows of ch sp(s).

6th inc row   4 ch; miss 1st ch sp; 1 tr into next tr;
work 6(6:7) more ch sp(s); 1 ch; miss next ch sp;
into next tr work 1 tr/1 ch/1 tr; * work 14(15:16)
more ch sp(s); 1 ch; miss next ch sp; into next tr
work 1 tr/1 ch/1 tr; repeat from * 7 times; continue
with ch sp(s) to end; – 144(153:162) ch sp(s); turn.
Work 6 more rows of ch sp(s).

7th inc row   4 ch; miss 1st ch sp; 1 tr into next tr;
work 6(7:7) more ch sp(s); 1 ch; miss next ch sp;

Day suit see instructions on page 11

Evening dress see instructions on page 32

into next tr work 1 tr/1 ch/1 tr; * work 15(16:17)
more ch sp(s); 1 ch; miss next ch sp; into next tr
work 1 tr/1 ch/1 tr; repeat from * 7 times; continue
with ch sp(s) to end; 153(162:171) ch sp(s); turn.
Work 5 more rows of ch sp(s) or as many as
required.

Sleeves (both alike)

Work in rounds.

1st round   rejoin yarn under arm in sp between 2
tr; 4 ch; 1 tr into next sp; 1 ch; work 2 tr together
(inserting hook into centre tr and 3rd tr of cluster);
continue with ch sp(s) to within next cluster; work
2 tr together (inserting hook into 1st and centre tr
of cluster) 1 ch; 1 tr into next sp; 1 ch; ss into 3rd
of 4 ch; – 34(37:40) ch sp(s); turn.

2nd round   4 ch; miss 1st ch sp; 1 tr into next tr;
1 ch; work 2 tr together (inserting hook into each
of next 2 tr, miss ch sp between); continue with
ch sp(s) to within 3rd tr from end; 1 ch; work 2 tr
together; 1 ch; miss next ch sp; 1 tr into next tr;
1 ch; ss into 3rd of 4 ch; – 32(35:38) ch sp(s); turn.
Work 23 more rounds of ch sp(s).

Dec round   4 ch; miss 1st ch sp; 1 tr into next tr;
work 3(4:5) more ch sp(s); 1 ch; miss next ch sp;
work 2 tr together; * 1 ch; work 8(9:9) more ch
sp(s); 1 ch; miss next ch sp; work 2 tr together;
repeat from * once; continue with ch sp(s) to end;
ss into 3rd of 4 ch; 29(32:35) ch sp(s); turn.
Work 9 more rounds of ch sp(s) or as many as
required. Fasten off.

To make up

Tassels (instructions pages 115–117, *see* Fringe)
Each strand measures 15cm (6in.). Use 2 strands
for each tassel. To cut a number of strands at
once, wind each ball of yarn (one at a time) round
a longish piece of cardboard, measuring 7.5cm
(3in.) in height. Now cut along one edge.
* Begin in 1st row from the bottom and work
upwards. Work 1 tassel into each ch sp over next
2 rows. Now miss 2 rows. * Repeat from * to * 20
times.
Work 1 tassel into each ch sp over next 3 rows.
** Miss 1 row. Work 1 tassel into each ch sp of
next row**. Repeat, from ** to ** 6(6:7) times.
Fill in 0(1:0) further row.

Sleeves

Repeat from * to * 8 times. Fill in 3 more rows.
Join hook and eye to top neck corners.

Winter dress with standaway collar

Materials   32(34:36) balls of *Lister/Lee Target Kaftan*
crochet hook no 5.00

Measurements   to fit bust 81(86:91)cm
32(34:36)in.
Length from shoulder (adjustable)   107cm (42in.)
Sleeve length from under arm excluding turn up
cuff   43.5(45:46.5)cm   17(17¾:18¼)in.

Tension   8 tr and 7 rows of tr to 10cm (4in.)
pattern   22 st(s) to 13cm (5in.) and 5 rows to 5cm
(2in.)

Abbreviations/explanations   page 119

Make 208(220:232) ch.

Foundation row   1 tr into 4th ch from hook; 1 tr
into each of next ch to end; – 206(218:230) st(s);
turn.

The pattern

1st patt row   2 ch (to count as 1st tr); miss 1st tr;
★ 1 tr into next tr (insert hook from the front of the
work from right to left horizontally under the bar
of the tr of the previous row, the hook being at
the front of the work) ★; ★★ 1 tr into each of next
2 tr (now insert the hook from the back of the
work from right to left under the bar of the tr of
the previous row, the hook being at the back of
the work) ★★; repeat from ★ to ★ twice and ★★ to
★★ to end, work last tr into top ch; turn.

2nd patt row   2 ch (to count as 1st tr), miss 1st tr;
work 1 tr to the back of next tr; ★ work 1 tr to the
front of each of next 2 tr; work one tr to the back
of each of next 2 tr ★; repeat from ★ to ★ to end,
work last tr into 2nd ch; turn.

3rd patt row   2 ch (to count as 1st tr), miss 1st tr;
work 1 tr to the front of next tr; ★ work 1 tr to the
back of each of next 2 tr; work 1 tr to the front of
each of next 2 tr ★; repeat from ★ to ★ to end,
work last tr into 2nd ch; turn.
Work 17 more rows in pattern.

Shape back of neck

1st dec row   continue in pattern over 91(97:103)
st(s); ★ work 3 tr together (insert hook either to the
front or back, as required) ★; – 2 st(s) dec; turn.

2nd dec row   2 ch (these do not count as 1 tr);
repeat from ★ to ★ previous row; continue in
pattern to end; turn.
Work 6 more rows in pattern.

Shape front of neck

1st inc row   continue in pattern to within
90th(96th:102nd) st; 3 tr into next tr (ie 3rd ch) –
2 st(s) inc; turn.

2nd inc row   2 ch (to count as 1st tr); 2 tr into 1st
tr; continue in pattern to end. Fasten off.

Miss 18 st(s) and rejoining yarn in 1st of remaining
st(s) complete 2nd side to match 1st, reverse all
shaping. Do not fasten off at the end, but work 18
ch; join to 1st side with a ss into 1st st. Fasten off.

Next row   With wrong side of work facing rejoin
yarn at the beginning of row and continue in
pattern to within 1st ch; 1 tr into each of next ch;
continue in pattern to end; turn.
Work 14 more rows in pattern. Fasten off.

Skirt (length adjustable)

Work in rounds.

Next round   With wrong side of work facing
rejoin yarn in 104th(110th:116th) st from end; 3 ch
(to count as 1st tr); 1 tr into each of next 30(32:34)
tr; miss 72(74:76) st(s) of the front sleeve edge and
continue along this edge with 1 tr into each of
next 62(66:70) st(s); miss 72(74:76) st(s) of the back
sleeve edge and continue along this edge with 1 tr
into each of remaining 31(33:35) st(s); ss into 3rd
ch; – 124(132:140) st(s); turn.

Next round   3 ch (to count as 1st tr); 1 tr into
each of next tr to end; ss into 3rd ch; turn.
Work 26 more rounds of tr.

Next round   bring this tr round up to 128(136:144)
st(s) by inc 4 st(s) anywhere on the round; ss into
3rd ch; turn.

1st inc round   3 ch (to count as 1st tr); 1 tr into
each of next 6(7:7) tr; 2 tr into next tr; ★ 1 tr into
each of next 15(16:17) tr; 2 tr into next tr; repeat
from ★ 6 times; 1 tr into each of next tr to end; ss
into 3rd ch; (8 st(s) inc) – 136(144:152) st(s); turn.
Work 27 more rounds of tr, inc 8 st(s) on every 4th
round (ie on the next inc round work 2 tr into every
17th(18th:19th) st, on the next inc round in every

18th(19th:20th) st and so on; bearing in mind that on the very 1st inc of every inc round only half the number of st(s) (or as near to half as possible) are worked at the beginning of the round and the remainder at the end. Last round 184(192:200) st(s). Now work 2 rounds of dc. Fasten off.

Collar

Make 48 ch.

Foundation row   tr into 4th ch from hook; 1 tr into each of next ch to end; – 46 st(s); turn.

Now continue in pattern over next 53 rows. Fasten off.

Turn-up cuffs (length adjustable)

Rejoin yarn in corner st of lower sleeve edge with 3 ch (to count as 1st tr); now work 67 tr, evenly spaced, all along lower sleeve edge.

Continue in pattern over 14 more rows (or as many as required).

Next row   1 ch; 1 dc into each of next tr to end. Fasten off.

To make up

Join sleeve seams. Join collar to main part. Join collar seam.

Winter dress with toggle fastening

Materials   13(14:14:15) balls of *Pingouin Confortable* M
2(2:2:2) balls of *Pingouin Confortable* C
crochet hook no 4.00
2 toggles;

Measurements   to fit bust 81(86:91:96)cm
32(34:36:38)in.
Length from shoulder (excluding border) adjustable
112cm (44in.)
Border and turn up cuffs   5cm (2in.)
Sleeve length from under arm   46.5(46.5:47.75:
47.75)cm 18¼(18¼:18¾:18¾)in.

Tension   17 tr and 8 rows of tr to 10cm (4in.)

Abbreviations/explanations   *page 119*

Front bib

With M make 44 ch.

1st row   1 dc into 2nd ch from hook; 1 dc into
each of next 20 ch; 5 dc into next ch; 1 dc into
each of next ch to end; – 47 st(s); turn.

2nd row   1 ch; 1 dc into each of next 22 dc; 3 dc
– called 1 cluster – into next dc; 1 dc into next dc;
1 cluster into next dc; 1 dc into each of next dc to
end; turn.
Change to C.

3rd row   1 ch; * 1 dc into each of next dc to including 1st dc of next cluster; 1 cluster into next dc
(ie centre dc of cluster) *; repeat from * to * once;
1 dc into each of next dc to end; – 4 st(s) inc; turn.
In 2 row stripe sequence repeat previous row 5
times; last row 75 st(s).

Shape neck

Inc row   1 ch; 2 dc into 1st dc; repeat from * to *
3rd row twice; 1 dc into each of next dc to within
last dc; 2 dc into last dc; – 6 st(s) inc; turn.
Continue in 2 row stripe sequence repeat previous
row 7 times; last row 123 st(s). Fasten off.

Back bib

With M make 54 ch.

1st row   1 dc into 2nd ch from hook; 1 dc into
each of next 25 ch; 5 dc into next ch; 1 dc into
each of next ch to end; – 57 st(s); turn.

2nd row   1 ch; 1 dc into each of next 27 dc; 1
cluster into next dc; 1 dc into next dc; 1 cluster
into next dc; 1 dc into each of next dc to end;
turn.
Change to C.

In 2 row stripe sequence repeat 3rd front bib row
11 times; last row 105 st(s). Continue in 2 row stripe
sequence with 3 inc rows as for front bib; last row
123 st(s). Fasten off. Join centre seam. Now join
front to back bib at shoulder on the corner st(s) of
last row only.

Shoulder

1st row   With wrong side of work facing rejoin M
to back in centre dc of cluster with 3 ch (to count
as 1st tr); 1 tr into each of next dc to end (ie up
back bib and down front bib edge); 92 st(s);
turn.

Tr row   3 ch (to count as 1st tr) miss st under
hook; 1 tr into each of next tr to end, working
last tr into 3rd ch; turn.
Work 8(9:10:11) tr rows more. Fasten off.

Sleeves

Dec row   With wrong side of work facing rejoin
M in 15th(13th:11th:9th) st from beginning of previous row; 3 ch; work 2 tr together; 1 tr into each
of next tr to within 17th(15th:13th:11th) st from end;
work 3 tr together; – 60(64:68:72) st(s): turn.

Next dec row   3 ch (these do not count as 1 tr);
work 3 tr together; 1 tr into each of next tr to within
last 3 tr; work 3 tr together; – 4 st(s) dec; turn.
Repeat previous row once; 52(56:60:64) st(s).
Now work 35(35:36:36) tr rows more (or as many
as required).
Change to C and in 2 row stripe sequence work
10 rows of dc. Fasten off.

Complete 2nd side to match 1st, reverse all shaping. Fasten off. Join sleeve seams.

Skirt

Work in rounds.

1st round   Rejoin M in centre st of back bib row;
2 ch (to count as 1st dc); 1 dc into each of next dc
to including centre dc of cluster; now work
30(34:39:43) dc, evenly spaced, all along tr edge
to within centre dc of next cluster; 1 dc into each

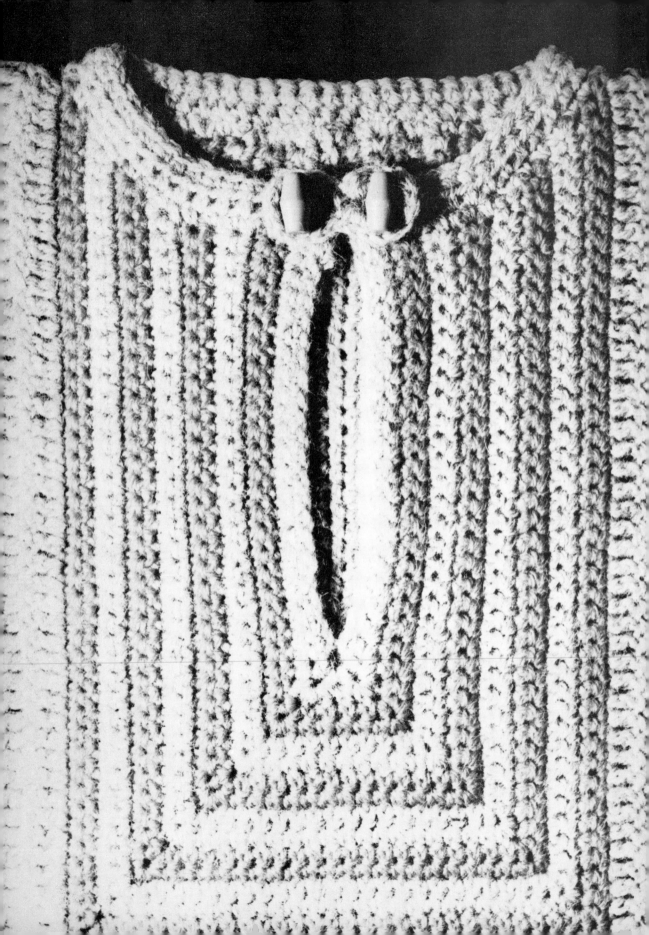

of next dc to including centre dc of next cluster (30:35:39:44) dc along tr edge to within centre dc of next cluster; 1 dc into each of next dc to end; ss into 2nd ch; − 126(135:144:153) st(s); turn.

Tr round   3 ch (to count as 1st tr); 1 tr into each of next dc to end; ss into 3rd ch; turn.
Work 18 tr rounds more.

1st inc round   3 ch (to count as 1st tr); 1 tr into each of next 5(6:6:7) tr; 2 tr into next tr; * 1 tr into each of next 13(14:15:16) tr; 2 tr into next tr *; repeat from * to * 7 times; 1 tr into each of next tr to end; ss into 3rd ch; − 9 st(s) inc; turn.

Work 40 more rounds (or as many as required) inc 9 st(s) on every 4th round (ie on next inc round work 2 tr in every 15th(16th:17th:18th) tr; on next inc round in every 16th(17th:18th:19th) tr and so on), bearing in mind that on the very 1st inc of every inc round only half (or as near to half as possible) the number of st(s) are worked at the beginning of the round and the remainder at the end; last round 234(243:252:261) st(s).
Change to C and in 2 row stripe sequence work 10 more rounds of dc. Fasten off.

Neck edge

1st row   With right side of work facing rejoin M in corner st of neck opening and work 56(56:60:60) dc, evenly spaced, all along neck edge; turn.

2nd row   2 ch; 1 htr into each of next dc to end; turn.
Add one more row of dc. Fasten off.

Fastening

Make 8 ch; ss to form a ring; make 8 more ch; ss into 8th ch to form an 8 shape; now work 15 dc into each ring; ss into 1st dc. Fasten off.

To make up

Sew toggles in place and join with fastening.

Sleeveless winter top

Materials   20(21:22) balls of *Wendy Sorbet*
crochet hooks nos 3.50 and 4.00

Measurements   small (medium, large)

Tension   8 tr to 5 cm (2in.) and 5 rows of tr to
7.5cm (3in.)

Abbreviations/explanations   page 119

Side 1 (front and back)

With hook no 4.00 make 173(175:177) loose ch for
side edge.

Foundation row   1 dc into 2nd ch from hook; 1 dc
into each of next 9 ch; 1 tr into each of next
152(154:156) ch; 1 dc into each of remaining 10 ch;
172(174:176) st(s); turn.
Next row   1 ch; 1 dc into each of next 10 dc; 1 tr
into each of next tr to within 1st dc; 1 dc into each
of next 10 dc; turn.
Repeat previous row 25(27:29) times more. Fasten
off.
Repeat above instructions for side 2.

To make up

Fold Side 1 in half and join along one side, leaving
a 30.5cm (12in.) opening for armholes. Repeat for
Side 2.

Now join Side 1 to Side 2 over 33cm (13in.) at the
Front and 46cm (18in.) at the Back.

With hook no 3.50 work 1 round of dc around
neck and lower edge.

Square-patterned winter top

Materials   29(30:32:33) balls of *Pingouin Iceberg* crochet hook no 6.00

Measurements   to fit bust 81(86:91:96)cm 32(34:36:38)in.
Length from shoulder seam   62.5cm (24½in.) for the 1st 2 sizes. 67.5cm (26½in.) for the last 2 sizes.
Sleeve length from under arm (adjustable)   51cm (20in.)

Tension   3 pattern (ie 9 st(s) to 8cm (3¼in.) and 4 pattern rows to 5cm (2in.)

Abbreviations/explanations   page 119

Front/Back (both alike)

Make 53(56:59:62) ch.
Foundation row   tr into 4th ch from hook; 1 tr into each of next ch to end; 51(54:57:60) st(s); turn.

The pattern

2nd row   3 ch (to count as 1st tr), miss st under hook; 1 tr into next tr (insert hook from the front of the work horizontally from right to left under the bar of the tr of previous row, the hook being at the front of the work); work 1 more tr in this way; 1 tr into next tr (now insert the hook from the back of the work from right to left under the bar of the tr of previous row); work 2 more tr in this way; continue like this working 3 tr under the front of the tr bar and 3 tr under the back of the tr bar to end, working last tr into 3rd ch; turn.

3rd row   3 ch (to count as 1st tr); miss st under

hook; work 1 tr to the back of each next 2 tr; work 1 tr to the front of each of next 3 tr; work 1 tr to the back of each of next 3 tr; continue in this way (ie reversing the check effect); last tr into 3rd ch; turn.

4th row   work as for 3rd row.

5th and 6th row   work as for 2nd row.
Repeat rows 3 to 6 10(10:11:11) times.
Repeat rows 3 and 4. Fasten off.

Sleeves (both alike)

Note   length adjustable.

Make 59 ch.

1st row   1 dc into each of next 10 ch; 1 tr into each of 48 ch; turn.

2nd row   work 2nd pattern row as for front/back to within 1st dc; ss into each of next 10 dc; turn.

3rd row   1 ch; 1 dc into each of next 10 ss (insert hook through the back ch, thus creating a ch at the front of the work); continue with 3rd pattern row to end; turn. Continue in pattern over the next 27(29:31:33) rows, always ending with ss into each of last 10 dc and dc into each of 10 ss at the beginning of each row.
Do not fasten off, but work 1 row of tr, evenly spaced, along top sleeve edge.
Fasten off.

To make up

Join sleeve seams. Join shoulder seams (leaving appropriate neck opening). Join sleeves to main part. Join side seams.

Winter top with contrasting sleeves

Materials   9(10:10) balls of *Madame Pingouin* M
1(1:1) ball of *Madame Pingouin* C
crochet hook no 4.00

Measurements   size small (medium: large)

Tension   9 tr to 5cm (2in.)   7 rows of tr to 8cm
$(3\frac{1}{4}$in.)

Abbreviations/explanations   page 119

For chevron pattern see pages 86 and 87.

Front/Back (both alike)

With M make 6 ch.

1st row   2 tr into 4th ch from hook; 3 tr into each
of next 2 ch; – 9 st(s); turn.

2nd row   3 ch (to count as 1st tr); 2 tr into 1st tr
(ie st immediately under hook); tr into each of next
3 tr; 5 tr – called 1 cluster – into next tr; tr into
each of next 3 tr; 3 tr into last st (ie 3rd ch); – 17
st(s); turn.

3rd row   3 ch (to count as 1st tr); 2 tr into 1st tr;
tr into each of next tr to including 2nd tr of cluster;
1 cluster into next tr (ie centre tr of cluster); tr into
each of next tr to within last st; 3 tr into 3rd ch;
– 8 st(s) inc; turn.
Repeat previous row 10(11:12) times, inc 8 st(s) on
every row; last row 105(113:121) st(s).

Next row   3 ch; miss 1st tr; work next 2 tr together; tr into each of next tr to including 2nd tr of
cluster; 1 cluster into next tr; tr into each of next
tr to within last 3 st(s); work 3 tr together (insert
hook into last 2 tr and 3rd ch); – 105(113:121) st(s);
turn.

Next row   3 ch (these do not count as 1 tr); work
1st, 2nd and 3rd tr together; tr into each of next
tr to including 2nd tr of cluster; 1 cluster into next
tr; tr into each of next tr to within last 3 tr; work 3
tr together; turn.

Repeat previous row 18(19:20) times in M, plus 1
row in C, noting that the number of st(s) does not
alter, as the 4 tr which are inc when working the
cluster are dec at the beginning and end of each
row.

Next row   C – 1 ch; 1 dc into each of next tr to
end. Fasten off.

Sleeves (both alike)

With M make 116(120:124) ch.

1st row   1 dc into each of next 25 ch; 1 tr into
each of remaining ch; 115(119:123) st(s); turn.

2nd row   3 ch (to count as 1st tr); miss st under
hook; tr into each of next tr to within dc; dc into
each of next dc; turn.

3rd row   C – 1 ch; dc into each of next dc; tr into
each of next tr; turn.

4th row   C – 1 ch; 1 dc into each of next tr and
dc to end; turn.

5th row   M – 1 ch; dc into each of next 25 dc; tr
into each of next dc to end; turn.

6th row   M – repeat 2nd row.
Repeat row 3–6 6(7:8) times. Fasten off.

To make up

Join side seams. Join sleeves to main part. Join
sleeve seams.

Lower edge

1st Round   With right side of work facing, rejoin
M in either side seam st and work 110(118:126) dc,
evenly spaced, along lower edge; ss into 1st dc;
turn.
Now work 2 more rounds of dc. Fasten off.

Lower sleeve edge

With right side of work facing rejoin C in seam st
and work 2 rounds of dc, evenly spaced, round
sleeve edge. Fasten off.

Collar

1st Round   With right side of work facing rejoin
M in centre st between sleeves; 1 dc into centre
st; ★ 3 dc to next 2 rows; 2 dc to next 2 rows;
repeat from ★ once; ★★ 3 dc to next 2 rows; 1 dc
to next 2 rows; repeat from ★★ 3(5:7) times; ★★★ 2
dc to next 2 rows; 3 dc to next 2 rows; repeat
from ★★★ twice; 1 dc into centre st; repeat from ★;
★★ and ★★★; 1 ss into centre st.

2nd Round   3 ch (to count as 1st tr); 2 tr into the
base of 3 ch; 1 tr into each of next dc to within
next centre st; 3 tr into centre st; 1 tr into each of

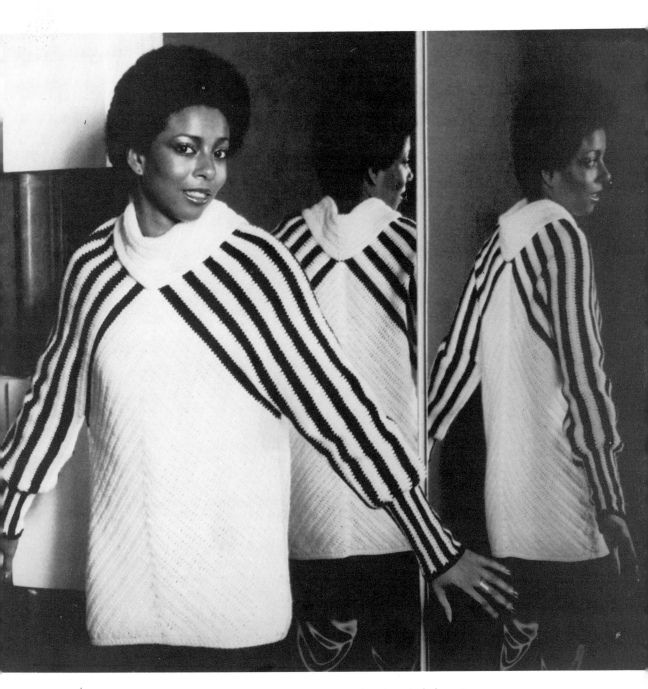

next dc to end; ss into 3rd ch; ss into next tr (ie centre st of tr group); – 70(74:78) st(s); turn.

3rd Round 3 ch (to count as 1st tr); 2 tr into the base of 3 ch; tr into each of next tr to including 1st tr of tr group; 3 tr into next tr; tr into each of next tr to end; ss into 3rd ch; ss into next tr; turn.

Repeat previous row 10 times more, always inc 4 st(s) on each round.

Next round 1 ch; 1 dc into each of next tr to end; ss into 1st dc. Fasten off.

⚓Granny square skirt

See colour section between pages 72 and 73

Materials 5(5:6) balls of *Pingouin Confortable* M (black)
3(3:3) balls of *Pingouin Confortable* C1 (red)
2(2:2) balls of *Pingouin Confortable* C2 (grey)
2(2:2) balls of *Pingouin Confortable* C3 (dark grey)
crochet hook no 4.00

Measurements small (medium: large)
Length (adjustable) 60cm (23½in.) stretch after pressing 6.5cm (2½in.)

Tension 9 tr to 5cm (2in.) 4 rows of tr to 5cm (2in.)

Abbreviations/explanations page 119

Note The length on this skirt is adjustable on the M tr rounds above and below stripe sequences

With M make 120(126:132) ch for waist edge; ss into 1st ch to form a ring.

1st round 2 ch (to count as 1st dc); 1 dc into each of next ch to end; ss into 2nd ch; – 120(126:132) st(s); turn.

2nd round 2 ch (to count as 1st dc); 1 dc into each of next dc to end of round; ss into 2nd ch; turn.
Work 6 more rounds of dc in 2-row stripe sequence C2,C3,C1.

Next round M – 3 ch (to count as 1st tr); 1 tr into each of next dc to end of round; ss into 3rd ch; turn.

1st skeleton shape

★ *1st row* 3 ch (these do not count as 1 tr); tr into each of next 17(18:19) tr; work 2 tr together – 18(19:20) st(s); turn.

2nd row 3 ch (these do not count as 1 tr); miss st under hook; 1 tr into each of next tr to within last 2 tr; work 2 tr together; – 2 st(s) dec; turn.
Repeat previous row 5 times; last row 6(7:8) st(s).

Next row 3 ch (to count as 1st tr); 2 tr into 1st tr; 1 tr into each of next tr to within last st; 3 tr into last tr; – 4 st(s) inc; turn.
Repeat previous row 6 times; last row 34(35:36) st(s). Fasten off.★

Rejoin M in next tr of remaining st(s) and repeat

from ★ to ★ 5 more times, always joining each finished skeleton shape to previous one with a ss; the last skeleton shape having to be joined at the beginning and end of last row to the adjoining ones.

Next round 3 ch (to count as 1st tr); 1 tr into each of next tr to end of round; ss into 3rd ch; 204(210:216) st(s); turn.

Now work 10 more rounds of dc in 2-row stripe sequence C1,C3,C2,C3,C1, change to M and work 3 more rounds of tr.

Repeat from ★ to ★ 1st skeleton shape 10 times, joining each shape as above.
Work 3 more rounds of tr; 1st round 340(350:360) st(s).

Continue with 10 more rounds of dc in the same 2-row stripe sequence as centre stripes.
Fasten off.

Granny square (make 16)

With C3 make 4 ch; ss into 1st ch to form a ring.

1st round 3 ch (to count as 1st tr); 2 tr into ring; ★ 1 ch; 3 tr into ring; repeat from ★ twice; 1 ch; ss into 3rd ch; turn.

2nd round C2 – 3 ch (to count as 1st tr); into 1st ch sp work 2 tr/1 ch/3 tr; ★ 1 ch; into next ch sp work 3 tr/1 ch/3 tr; repeat from ★ twice; 1 ch; ss into 3rd ch; turn.

3rd round 3 ch (to count as 1st tr); 2 tr into 1st ch sp; ★ 1 ch; into next ch sp work 3 tr/1 ch/3 tr; 1 ch; into next ch sp work 3 tr; repeat from ★ twice; 1 ch; into next ch sp work 3 tr/1 ch/3 tr; 1 ch; ss into 3rd ch; turn.

4th round C1 – 3 ch (to count as 1st tr); 2 tr into 1st ch sp; ★ 1 ch; into next ch sp (ie corner ch sp) work 3 tr/1 ch/3 tr; 1 ch/3 tr into each of next ch sp(s) to within next corner ch sp; repeat from ★ twice; 1 ch; into corner ch sp work 3 tr/1 ch/3 tr; 1 ch/3 tr into each of next ch sp to end; ss into 3rd ch; turn.
Repeat previous round once. Fasten off.

To make up

Join motifs into spaces and press skirt well with a damp cloth. Allow steam to disappear completely before removing cloth.

Take 3× 2.5cm (3× 100in.) lengths of M to make draw string (instructions page 118). Thread draw string through waist edge and tie in a bow at the back.

Poncho

Materials   40 balls of *Wendy Sorbet*
crochet hook no 4.00
1 pair of toggles

Measurements   one size (to fit bust 81(86:91)cm
32(34:36)in.

Tension   8 tr to 5cm (2in.) and 5 rows of tr to
7.5cm (3in.)

Abbreviations/explanations   page 119

Note   This poncho consists of 2 identical parts,
worked entirely in tr. The two parts are joined
together at the front and at the back and at the
shoulders.

Begin at neck and make 40 ch for neck edge.

1st row   2 tr into 4th ch from hook; 1 tr into each
of next 17 ch; 5 tr into next ch – called 1 cluster; 1
tr into each of next 17 ch; 3 tr into last ch; 45 st(s);
turn.

2nd row   3 ch (to count as 1st tr); 2 tr into 1st tr;
1 tr into each of next tr to including 2nd tr of
cluster; 1 cluster into next tr (ie centre tr); 1 tr into
each of next tr to within last tr (ie 3 ch); 3 tr into
3rd of 3 ch; – 8 st(s) inc; turn.
Repeat previous row 4 times more; last row 85
st(s).

Next row   3 ch (to count as 1st tr), miss st under
hook; 1 tr into each of next tr to including 2nd tr
of cluster; 1 cluster into next tr; 1 tr into each of

next tr to end, work last tr into 3rd of 3 ch; – 4
st(s) inc; turn.
Repeat previous row 24 times more; last row 185
st(s).

Next row   3 ch (to count as 1st tr), miss st under
hook; 1 tr into each of next tr to within cluster;
work next 3 tr together (ie 1st, 2nd and 3rd tr of
cluster); – 91 st(s); turn.

Next row   3 ch (these do not count as 1 tr, do not
miss under hook); work 3 tr together; 1 tr into
each of next tr to end, work last tr into 3rd of 3
ch; – 2 st(s) dec; turn.

Next row   3 ch (to count as 1st tr) miss st under
hook; 1 tr into each of next tr to within last 3 st(s);
work 3 tr together; – 2 st(s) dec; turn.
Repeat previous 2 rows alternately until all st(s)
are dec (ie 43 more rows of tr). Fasten off.

To work other side, rejoin yarn with right side of
work facing in centre tr of cluster with 3 ch; work
centre tr, 4th and 5th tr together and continue as
for 1st side reverse all shaping. Do not fasten off, but
work 1 round of dc, evenly spaced, (approx 2 dc to
each row) along all edges; work 3 dc into corner
st(s). Fasten off.
Repeat complete instructions for 2nd part.

To make up

Join shoulder and back seams. Join front seam,
leaving a 22cm (8½in.) neck opening. Sew toggles
to the front opening.

Mexican type skirt

Materials 8(8:9) balls of *Pingouin Poudreuse* M
2(2:2) balls of *Pingouin Poudreuse* C
crochet hook no 4.00
waist measure of 2.5cm (1in.) elastic
15cm (6in.) zip fastener

Measurements size 10(12:14)
Length from waist to tip (excluding fringe)
89.5(91:92)cm; 35¼(35¾:36¼)in.

Tension 17 tr and 8 rows to 10cm (4in.)

Abbreviations/explanations page 119

For chevron pattern see pages 86 and 87.

Front/Back (both alike)

With M make 6 ch.

1st row 2 tr into 4th ch from hook; 3 tr into each
of next 2 ch; turn.

2nd row 3 ch (to count as 1st tr); 2 tr into 1st tr
(ie st immediately under hook); 1 tr into each of
next 3 tr; 5 tr – called 1 cluster – into next tr; 1 tr
into each of next 3 tr; 3 tr into last tr (ie 3rd ch); –
17 st(s); turn.

3rd row 3 ch (to count as 1st tr); 2 tr into 1st tr;
1 tr into each of next tr to including 2nd tr of
cluster; 1 cluster into next tr (ie centre tr of cluster);
1 tr into each of next tr to within last st; 3 tr into
last st (ie 3rd ch); – 8 st(s) inc; turn.
Repeat previous row 6(7:8) times more, last row
73(81:89) st(s); turn.

Shape sides

Next row 3 ch (these do not count as 1 tr); work
1st, 2nd and 3rd tr together; 2 tr into next tr; 1 tr
into each of next tr to including 2nd tr of cluster;
1 cluster into next tr; 1 tr into each of next tr to
within 4th st from end; 2 tr into next tr; work last
3 tr together; – 75(83:91) st(s); turn.
Repeat previous row 28 times in M, once in C,
once in M; last row 135(143:151) st(s).

Heart motif border

Note When changing colour, finish preceding tr
in the new colour (ie the last 2 loops on hook).
Leave yarn attached and carry it along at the base
of row when not in use, working over it in the new
colour.

Next row M – 3 ch; work 1st 3 tr together; 2 tr
into next tr; 1 tr into each of next 4(5:6) tr; * C – 4
tr; M – 3 tr; C – 4 tr; M – 4(5:6) tr*; repeat from *
to * twice; C – 4 tr; M – 3 tr; C – 4 tr; M – 3 tr
plus 1st of cluster tr; C – next 3 cluster tr; M – 5th
cluster tr plus next 3 tr; repeat from * to * 3 times
C – 4 tr; M – 3 tr; C – 4 tr; carrying C along at the
base of row M – 4(5:6) tr, 2 tr into next tr; work
last tr together; now twist C once round M to
bring up to next level and continue carrying at the
base of row; turn.

Next row M – 3 ch; work 1st 3 tr together; 2 tr
into next tr; 1 tr into each of next 2(3:4) tr; * C – 6
tr; M – 1 tr; C – 6 tr; M – 2(3:4) tr *; repeat from *
to * twice; C – 6 tr; M – 1 tr; C – 6 tr; M – 3 tr;
C – 1 tr/cluster/1 tr; M – 3 tr; repeat from * to * 3
times; C – 6 tr; M – 1 tr; C – 6 tr; M – 2(3:4) tr; 2 tr
into next tr; work last 3 tr together; turn.

Next row M – 3 ch; work 1st 3 tr together; 2 tr
into next tr; 1 tr into each of next 1(2:3) tr; * C –
13 tr; M – 2(3:4) tr *; repeat from * to * twice;
C – 13 tr; M – 3 tr; C – 3 tr/cluster/3 tr; M – 3 tr;
repeat from * to * 3 times; C – 13 tr; M – 1(2:3) tr;
2 tr into next tr; work last 3 tr together; turn.

Next row M – 3 ch; work 1st 3 tr together; 2 tr
into next tr; 1(2:3) tr; * C – 11 tr; M – 4(5:6) tr *;
repeat from * to * twice; C – 11 tr; M – 4 tr; C –
5 tr/clusters/5 tr; M-4 tr; repeat from * to * 3
times; C – 11 tr; M – 1(2:3) tr; 2 tr into next tr;
work last 3 tr together; turn.

Next row M – 3 ch; work 1st 3 tr together; 2 tr
into next tr; 2(3:4) tr; * C – 7 tr; M – 8(9:10) tr*;
repeat from * to * twice; C – 7 tr; M – 7 tr; C – 6
tr; M – cluster; C – 6 tr; M – 7 tr; repeat from * to
* 3 times; C – 7 tr; M – 2(3:4) tr; 2 tr into next tr;
work last 3 tr together; turn.

Next row M – 3 ch; work 1st 3 tr together; 2 tr
into next tr; 3(4:5) tr; * C – 3 tr; M – 12(13:14) tr *;
repeat from * to * twice; C – 3 tr; M – 10 tr; C – 4
tr; M – 3 tr/cluster/3 tr; C – 4 tr; M – 10 tr; repeat
from * to * 3 times; C – 3 tr; M – 3(4:5) tr; 2 tr into
next tr; work last 3 tr together; fasten off C; turn.
Work 3 more tr rows as above in colour sequence
M,C,M.

Next row 3 ch; miss 2 tr; 1 dc into next tr; * 2
fairly loose ch; miss 2 tr; 1 dc into next tr; repeat

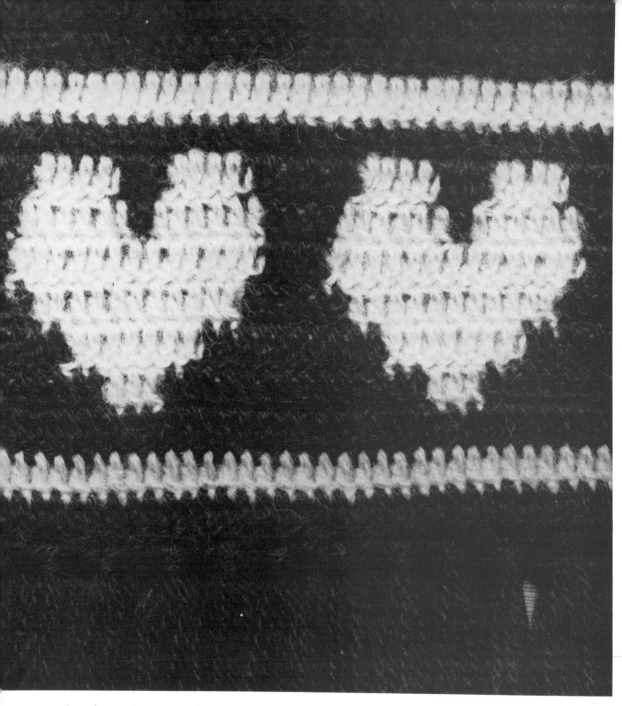

from * to end, missing only 1 tr over cluster. Fasten off.

Tassels

Take 5 strands of M 15cm (6in.) long and put 1 tassel into each ch sp. For fringe instructions turn to pages 115–117.

To make up

Join sides, leaving a 15cm (6in.) opening on one side. Before joining in zip fastener, work 1 round of dc, evenly spaced, round waist edge and side opening. Sew in zip fastener and join elastic to waist edge.

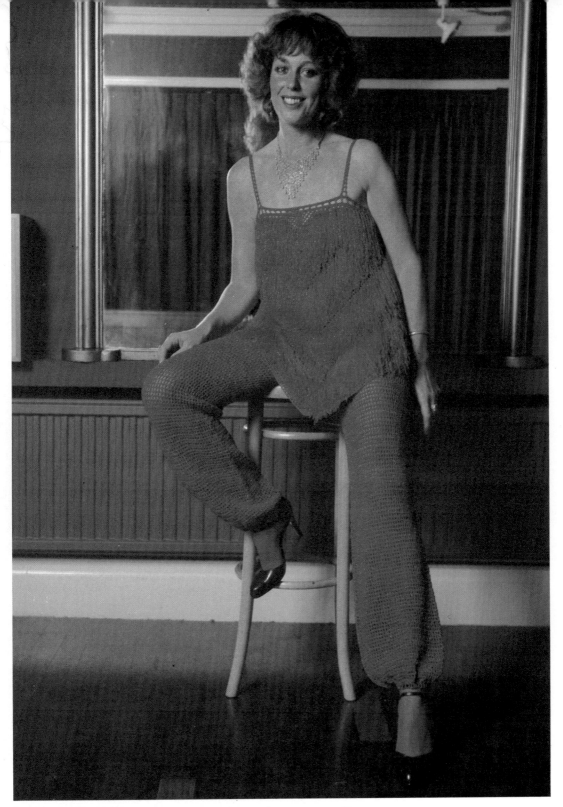

Evening outfit with harem trousers see instructions on page 46

Granny square skirt see instructions on page 64

Waistcoat

Materials 8(8:9:9) balls of *Sirdar Palamino*
crochet hook no 5.00
two 50cm (19¾in) lengths of silk cord

Measurements to fit bust 81(86:91:96)cm
32(34:36:38)in.
Length from shoulder (excluding border) 40(43:
46:49)cm 15¾(17:18:19¼)in.

Tension 7 st(s) to 5cm (2in.) 5 rows of tr to
7.5cm (3in.)

Abbreviations/explanations page 119

Front (make 2)

make 47(51:55:59) ch.

Foundation row 1 tr into 4th ch from hook; 1 tr
into each of next ch to end; – 45(49:53:57) st(s);
turn.

Tr row 3 ch (to count as 1st tr) miss st under
hook; 1 tr into each of next tr to end, working
last tr into 3rd ch; turn.
Work 12(13:14:15) more rows of tr. Fasten off.

Back

As for front to including 14th(15th:16th:17th) row.
Next row 3 ch (to count as 1st tr) miss st under
hook; 1 tr into each of next 31(35:39:43) tr; miss
remaining st(s); 15 ch; turn.

Next row tr into 4th ch from hook; 1 tr into each
of next 11 ch; 1 tr into each of next tr to end; turn.
Work 13(14:15:16) more rows of tr. Fasten off.

To make up

Join shoulder and side seams, leaving appropriate
opening for armholes.
Rejoin yarn in corner st of lower edge and work
88(95:102:109) tr, evenly spaced, all along lower
edge.
Work 1 more row of tr. Fasten off.
Thread silk cord through each lower front corner
st(s), cross over front and tie each cord in a bow,
threading through the appropriate space of the
lower edge underneath.

Wedding dress

Materials 19 balls of *Pingouin Ritournelle*
crochet hook no 3.00
1 zip fastener 18cm (7in.) long
2m (75in.) ribbon

Measurements to fit bust 83.5/86/88.5cm
33/34/35in.
Length from waist (adjustable) 109cm (43¾in.)
Sleeve length adjustable on cuff only

Tension 12 tr to 5cm (2in.) and 11 rows to 10cm
(4in.)
one diamond measures 6.25 by 8.5cm (2½ by
3½in.)

Abbreviations/explanations page 119

Top

Make 74 ch for back waist edge.

1st row 2 tr into 4th ch from hook; ★ 3 ch; miss
2 ch; 1 dc into each of next 2 ch; 1 Pc st into next
ch; 1 dc into each of next 2 ch; 3 ch; miss 2 ch;
1 tr into each of next 3 ch ★; repeat from ★ to ★
to end, working 3 tr into last ch; – 6 patterns;
turn.

2nd row 4 ch; 2 tr into 1st tr (ie st immediately
under hook); 3 ch; miss 1 tr; 3 tr into next tr; ★ 3
ch; miss 3 ch sp and 1st dc; 1 dc into each of
next dc/Pc st/dc; 3 ch; miss next dc and 3 ch sp;
3 tr into next tr; 3 ch; miss 1 tr; 3 tr into next tr ★;
repeat from ★ to ★ to end, work last 3 tr into 4th
ch; turn.

3rd row 4 ch; 2 tr into 1st tr; 3 ch; miss 2 tr; 1 tr
into 3 ch sp; 3 ch; miss 2 tr; 3 tr into next tr; ★ 3
ch; miss 3 ch sp and 1st dc; 1 tr into next dc (ie
centre dc); 3 ch; miss next dc and 3 ch sp; 3 tr
into next tr; 3 ch; miss 2 tr; 1 tr into 3 ch sp; 3 ch;
miss 2 tr; 3 tr into next tr ★; repeat from ★ to ★ to
end, work last 3 tr into 4th ch; turn.

4th row 4 ch; 2 tr into 1st tr; 3 ch; miss 2 tr; 1 dc
each into next 3 ch sp/tr/3 ch sp; 3 ch; miss 2 tr;
3 tr into next tr; ★ 1 ch; miss next two 3 ch sp(s);
3 tr into next tr; 3 ch; miss 2 tr; 1 dc each into
next 3 ch sp/tr/3 ch sp; 3 ch; miss 2 tr; 3 tr into
next tr ★; repeat from ★ to ★ to end, work last 3 tr
into 4th ch; turn.

5th row 4 ch; 2 tr into 1st tr; 3 ch; miss 2 tr; 1 dc

each into 3 ch sp and 1st dc; Pc st into next dc
(ie centre dc); 1 dc each into next dc and 3 ch sp;
3 ch; miss 3 tr; 3 tr into 1 ch sp; ★ 3 ch; miss 3 tr;
1 dc each into 3 ch sp and 1st dc; Pc st into next
dc; 1 dc each into next dc and 3 ch sp; 3 ch; miss
3 tr; 3 tr into 1 ch sp ★; repeat from ★ to ★ to end,
work last 3 tr into 4th ch; turn.
Repeat 2nd to 5th row 10 times.

Shape front waist and neck edge

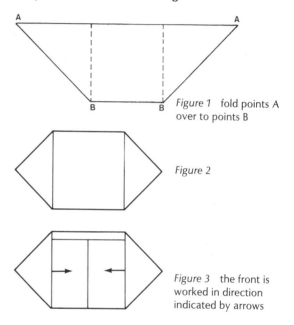

Figure 1 fold points A
over to points B

Figure 2

Figure 3 the front is
worked in direction
indicated by arrows

1st sh row 4 ch; miss 1st 2 tr; 3 tr into next tr;
repeat from ★ to ★ 2nd row 5 times; 3 ch; miss 3
ch and 1st dc; 1 dc into each of next dc/Pc st/dc;
3 ch; miss dc and 3 ch sp; 3 tr into next tr; 1 ch;
miss 1 tr; 1 tr into next tr; turn.

2nd sh row 6 ch; miss ch sp and 2 tr; 3 tr into
next tr; repeat from ★ to ★ 3rd row 5 times; 3 ch;
miss 3 ch sp and dc; 1 tr into next dc; 3 ch; miss
dc and 3 ch sp; 3 tr into next tr; 3 ch; miss 2 tr;
1 tr into 3rd of 4 ch; turn.

3rd sh row 1 ch; 1 dc each into 1st tr and 3 ch sp;
3 ch; miss 2 tr; 3 tr into next tr; repeat from ★ to ★
4th row 5 times; 1 ch; miss next two 3 ch sp(s);
3 tr into next tr; 3 ch; miss next 2 tr; 1 dc each
into 3 ch sp and 3rd of 6 ch; turn.

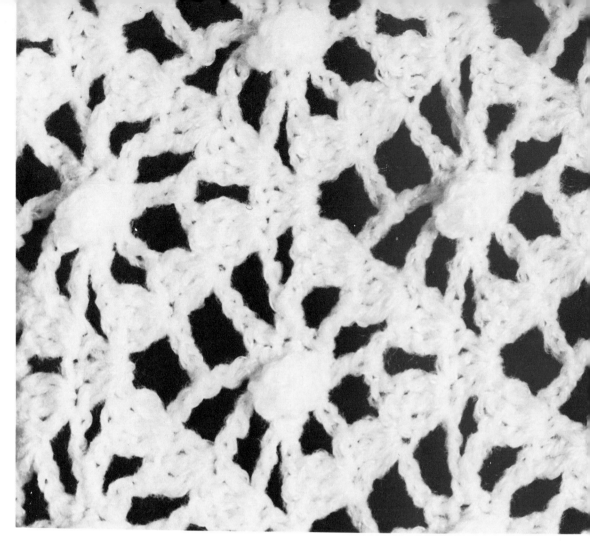

4th sh row   3 ch; Pc st into 1st dc; 1 dc into each of next dc and 3 ch sp; 3 ch; miss 3 tr; 3 tr into 1 ch sp; repeat from ★ to ★ 5th row 5 times; 3 ch; miss 3 tr; 1 dc each into next 3 ch sp and 2 dc; turn.

5th sh row   1 ch; 1 dc each into next 2 dc; 3 ch; miss next dc and 3 ch sp; 3 tr into next tr; 3 ch; miss 1 tr; 3 tr into next tr; repeat from ★ to ★ 2nd row 5 times; 3 ch; miss 3 ch sp and 1 dc; 1 dc each into next dc and Pc st; turn.

6th sh row   6 ch; miss 2 dc and 3 ch sp; 3 tr into next tr; 3 ch; miss 2 tr; 1 tr into 3 ch sp; 3 ch; miss 2 tr; 3 tr into next tr; repeat from ★ to ★ 3rd row 5 times; 3 ch; miss 3 ch sp and 1st dc; 1 tr into last dc; turn.

7th sh row   4 ch; miss 1st tr and 3 ch sp; 3 tr into next tr; 3 ch; miss 2 tr; 1 dc into each of next 3 ch sp/tr/3 ch sp; 3 ch; miss 2 tr; 3 tr into next tr; repeat from ★ to ★ 4th row 5 times; 1 ch; 1 tr into

3rd of 6 ch; turn.

8th sh row   3 ch (to count as 1st tr); 2 tr into 1 ch sp; repeat from ★ to ★ 5th row 6 times, work last 3 tr into 4 ch sp; turn.
Repeat 1st to 8th sh row once. Fasten off.
To work other side rejoin yarn with right side of work facing in 1st tr of 7th 3 tr group from end and repeat 1st to 8th sh row once, now repeat 1st to 7th sh row once. Fasten off.
Fold over sides to meet at the front and invisibly join (see figure 3).

Skirt

1st row   With right side of work facing rejoin yarn in corner st of right front waist edge and work 80 dc, evenly spaced, along front waist edge, now work 80 dc, evenly spaced, along back waist edge, thus joining front to back under arm on one side; turn.

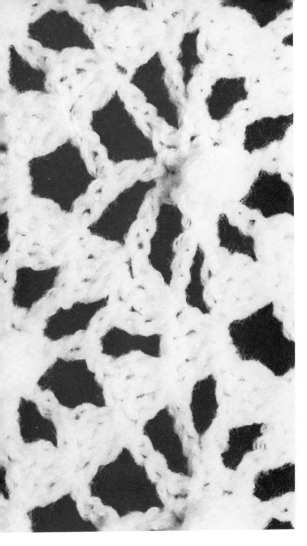

next 17 tr; 2 tr into next tr; repeat from * 8 times; 1 tr into each of remaining tr; ss into 1st st (ie 3rd ch); – 190 st(s); turn.

Work 57 more rounds of tr (or as many as required), inc 10 st(s) twice on every 4th round and thereafter 10 st(s) on every 5th round (ie on next inc round work 2 tr in every 19th tr, on next inc round 2 tr in every 20th tr and so on, bearing in mind that on the very 1st inc of every inc round only half the number of st(s) of the inc are worked at the beginning of the round and the remainder at the end), last inc round 300 st(s).

Note To shorten the length of the skirt adjust on the number of rounds worked in between inc rounds; to lengthen just add the appropriate number of rounds after the last inc round.

Last inc round 3 ch (to count as 1st tr); 1 tr into each of next 6 tr; 2 tr into next tr; * 1 tr into each of next 14 tr; 2 tr into next tr; repeat from * 18 times; 1 tr into each of remaining tr; ss into 3rd ch; – 320 st(s); turn.

Next round 5 ch; miss 1st tr; * 1 tr into next tr; 2 ch; miss next tr; repeat from * to end; ss into 3rd of 5 ch; – 160 ch sp(s) made; turn.

Next round 5 ch; miss ch sp; * 1 tr into next tr; 2 ch; miss ch sp; repeat from * to end; ss into 3rd of 5 ch; turn.
Work 11 more rounds of ch sp(s).

Inc round work 4 ch sp(s); inc 1 ch sp in next tr (ie work 1 tr/2 ch/1 tr); * work 9 ch sp(s); 2 ch; inc 1 ch sp in next tr; repeat from * 14 times; work ch sp(s) to end; ss into 3rd of 5 ch; – 176 ch sp(s); turn.
Work 12 more rounds of ch sp(s).

Next inc round work 5 ch sp(s); 2 ch; inc 1 ch sp in next tr; * work 10 ch sp(s); 2 ch; inc 1 ch sp in next tr; repeat from * 14 times; ch sp(s) to end; ss into 3rd of 5 ch; – 192 ch sp(s); turn.
Work 12 more rounds of ch sp(s). Fasten off.

Lacy border (make 3)

Make 31 ch.

1st row 1 tr into 4th ch from hook; 1 tr into next ch; * 1 ch; miss 1 ch; 1 tr into next ch; 1 ch; miss 1 ch; 1 tr into each of next 3 ch; repeat from * once; ** 1 ch; miss 1 ch; 1 tr into next ch; repeat from ** to end; turn.

2nd row 4 ch; miss 1st tr and ch sp; 1 tr into next tr; * 1 ch; miss ch sp; 1 tr into next tr; repeat

2nd row 3 ch (to count as 1st tr); miss 1st dc; 1 tr into each of next dc to end; turn.
Work 2 more rows of tr, always work last tr into top ch of previous row.

1st inc row 3 ch (to count as 1st tr); 1 tr into each of next 6 tr; 2 tr into next tr; * 1 tr into each of next 15 tr; 2 tr into next tr; repeat from * 8 times; 1 tr into each of remaining tr; – 170 st(s); turn.
Work 3 more rows of tr.

2nd inc row 3 ch (to count as 1st tr); 1 tr into each of next 7 tr; 2 tr into next tr; * 1 tr into each of next 16 tr; 2 tr into next tr; repeat from * 8 times; 1 tr into each of remaining tr; – 180 st(s); turn.
Work 3 more rows of tr.
Now continue working in rounds.

Inc round 3 ch (to count as 1st tr); 1 tr into each of next 8 tr; 2 tr into next tr; * 1 tr into each of

from * 3 times; ** 1 ch; miss ch sp and tr; 3 tr into next ch sp; 1 ch; miss 2 tr; 1 tr into next tr; repeat from ** once; 1 ch; miss ch sp and tr; 3 tr into next ch sp; 3 ch; miss next 2 tr; 3 tr into last st (ie 3rd ch); turn.

3rd row 4 ch (to count as 1st tr); 2 tr into 1st tr (ie st immediately under hook); 3 ch; miss 2 tr; 1 tr into 3 ch sp; 3 ch; miss 3 tr; 3 tr into next ch sp; * 1 ch; miss next tr and ch sp; 1 tr into 1st of 3 tr; 1 ch; 3 tr into next ch sp; repeat from * once; repeat from * 2nd row to end, work last tr into 3rd of 4 ch; turn.

4th row 4 ch; miss 1st tr and ch sp; 1 tr into next tr; repeat from * 2nd row once; repeat from ** 2nd row twice; 1 ch; miss ch sp and tr; 3 tr into next ch sp; 3 ch; miss next 3 tr; 1 dc into each of next 3 ch sp/tr/3 ch sp; 3 ch; miss next 2 tr; 3 tr into last st; turn.

5th row 4 ch (to count as 1st tr); 2 tr into 1st tr; 3 ch; miss 2 tr; 1 dc into each of next 3 ch sp and dc; Pc st into dc (ie centre dc); 1 dc into each of next dc and 3 ch sp; 3 ch; miss next 3 tr; 3 tr into next ch sp; repeat from * 3rd row twice; repeat from * 2nd row to end, working last tr into 3rd of 4 ch; turn.

6th row 4 ch; miss 1st tr and ch sp; 1 tr into next tr; 1 ch; miss ch sp; 1 tr into next tr; * 1 ch; miss next ch sp; 1 tr into 1st of 3 tr; 1 ch; 3 tr into next ch sp; repeat from * once; 1 ch; miss next ch sp; 1 tr into 1st of 3 tr; 1 ch; miss 1 tr; 3 tr into next tr (ie 3rd of 3 tr); ** 3 ch; miss 3 ch sp and 1st dc; 1 dc into each of next dc/Pc st/dc; 3 ch; miss next dc and 3 ch sp; work 3 tr together (insert hook twice into 2nd of 3 tr and once into 3rd ch); turn.

7th row 4 ch; work 2 tr together; 3 ch; miss 3 ch sp and dc; 1 tr into next dc (ie centre dc); 3 ch; miss next dc and 3 ch sp; 3 tr into 1st of 3 tr; 1 ch; miss next tr; 1 tr into next tr; 1 ch; miss next ch sp and tr; 3 tr into next ch sp; 1 ch; miss 2 tr; 1 tr into next tr; repeat from * once; repeat from * 2nd row to end; turn.

8th row 4 ch; miss 1st tr and ch sp; 1 tr into next tr; repeat from * 2nd row 3 times; repeat from * 6th row twice; 1 ch; miss ch sp; 1 tr into 1st of 3 tr; 1 ch; 3 tr into 3rd of 3 tr; 1 ch; miss next two 3 ch sp(s); work 3 tr together (insert hook 3 times into last st); turn.

9th row 4 ch; 1 tr into 1st st; 1 tr into ch sp; 1 ch; miss 2 tr; 1 tr into next tr; * 1 ch; miss ch sp and tr; 3 tr into next ch sp; 1 ch; miss 2 tr; 1 tr into

next tr; repeat from * once; repeat from * 2nd row to end of row; turn.
Repeat 2nd to 9th row 19 times for 1st border; 21 times for 2nd border and 23 times for 3rd border. Do not fasten off at the end, but work picot edging along zigzag edge.

Work 1 picot as follows: * 3 ch; 1 dc into the 1st of these 3 ch; 1 dc into zigzag edge; repeat from * to end (ie work 1 picot to each row, plus 1 extra picot into each of the points).
Join each border to form a circle. Now join 1st border to 1st ch sp row, 2nd border to 14th ch sp row and 3rd border to 27th ch sp row. The number of 2 ch sp(s) of the rows to be joined to should correspond to the number of rows worked on the borders.

Sleeves (both alike)
The length of the sleeve can only be adjusted on the cuff.
Work as for top to including 1st row.
Now repeat 1st to 8th Sh row 4 times.

Next row 1 ch; 1 dc into 1st tr; * miss next 2 tr; 2 dc into 3 ch sp; miss 1 dc; 1 dc into each of next dc and Pc st; miss 2 dc; 2 dc into 3 ch sp; miss 2 tr; 1 dc into next tr; repeat from * to end; 46 dc; turn.

1st dec row 1 ch; 1 dc into each of next 5 dc; work 2 dc together; * 1 dc into each of next 9 dc; work 2 dc together; repeat from * twice; 1 dc into each of remaining 6 dc; − 42 st(s); turn.
Work 1 row of dc.

2nd dec row 1 ch; 1 dc into each of next 2 dc; work 2 dc together; * 1 dc into each of next 4 dc; work 2 dc together; repeat from * 5 times; 1 dc into each of remaining 2 dc; − 35 st(s); turn.
Work 8 more rows of dc.

Picot edging
Next row 3 ch; 1 dc into 1st of these 3 ch; miss 1 dc; 1 dc into next dc; * 3 ch; 1 dc into 1st of these 3 ch; miss 2 dc; 1 dc into next dc; repeat from * to end; − 12 picots; fasten off.

To make up
Set in sleeves to match up with pattern on main part as much as possible. Join side seams; leaving an opening of 18cm (7in.). Join sleeve seams.
Work 1 round of dc, evenly spaced, round neck and side opening. Join in zip fastener. Tie ribbon round waist.

Crochet hints

Beginning and end of row

Figure 1 demonstrates the beginning of a treble row. In the text this would read: 3 ch (to count as 1st tr), miss st under hook; 1 tr into each of next . . . etc

Figure 2 demonstrates the end of a treble row. In the text this would read: . . . working last tr into last tr (ie 3rd ch)

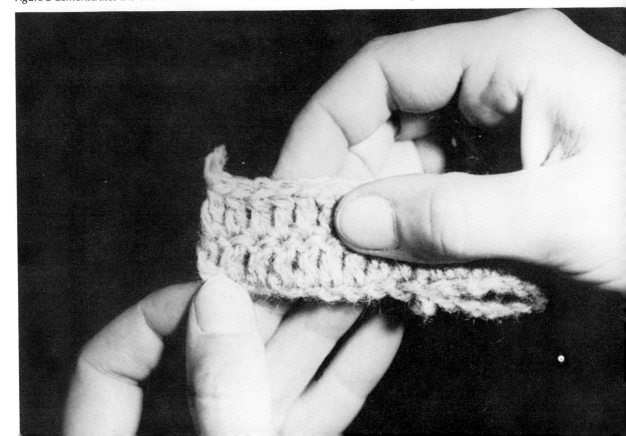

Tension

One of the most important factors for successful crochet is tension. In my own experience I have found that to change to a larger or smaller crochet hook to obtain the correct tension is not always the ultimate answer. The work can actually be made looser or tighter, as the case may be, if one point is borne in mind: it is the first loop that defines the tension. By working this loop looser (figure 1) or tighter (figure 2) the correct tension can be obtained without having to change the hook. Ideally this first loop should just enclose the hook (figure 2). The difference between a tight and a loose loop can be seen on figure 3, front view and figure 4, top view.

A similar situation arises with the height of a row, this again being part of correct tension. In this case it is the last loop that makes a small stitch (figure 4). The hook is held in a diagonal way, thus creating a tight third loop. A large stitch is created by keeping this last loop very loose, in other words, the hook is held horizontally (figure 5). The difference between a tightly worked last loop and a loosely worked last loop can be seen in figure 6. A loosely worked last loop can save up to one row in each five. Figure 7 contrasts the variations in tension illustrated in figures 5 and 6.

Figure 1

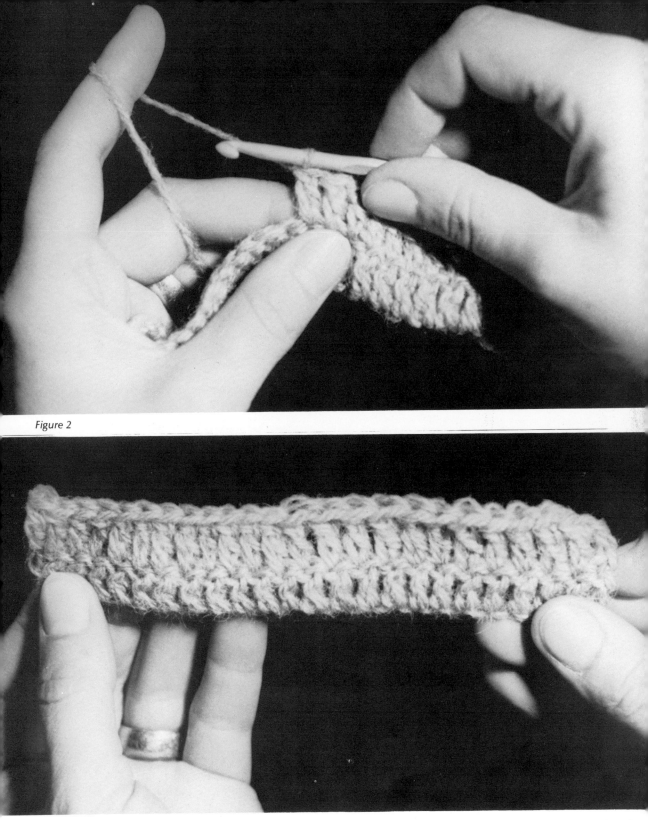

Figure 2

Figure 3

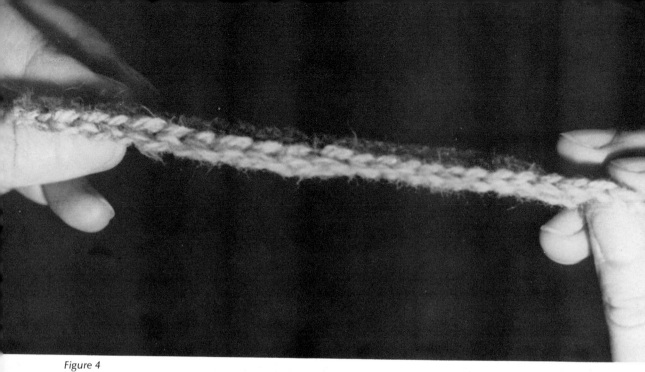

Figure 4

Figure 5

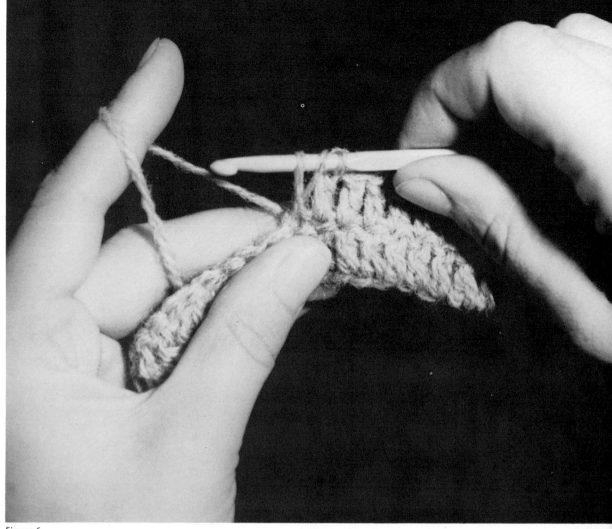

Figure 6

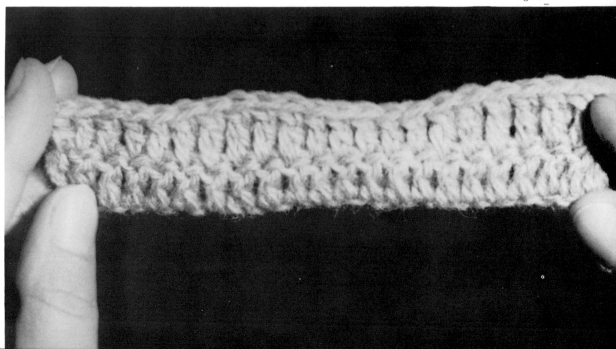

Figure 7

hevrons

When working chevrons, pull work gently towards
cluster (ie to the left up to cluster and to the right
once cluster is worked). This helps to keep the
lower edge straight.

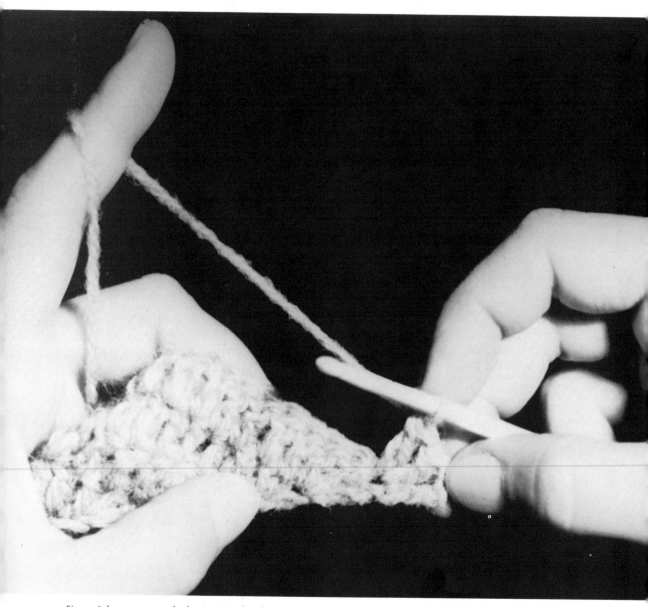

Figure 1 demonstrates the beginning of a chevron row. In the text this would read: 3 ch (to count as 1st tr); 2 tr into
1st tr (ie st immediately under hook)

Figure 2 demonstrates the end of a chevron row. In the text this would read: 1 tr into each of next tr to within last st (or tr); 3 tr into last st (ie 3rd ch)

Seams

The most natural way is, of course, to crochet seams together. To obtain a really finished look, it is important to bear a few points in mind. The natural gaps that occur between stitches, no matter how lacy the pattern should always be maintained on the seam as well. This means that we join the stitches on the seam only on those points where they join naturally on the pattern. On a tr row this works out as follows: ss through the tr of both layers of work; * 2 ch; ss through the base of the tr of both layers of work; repeat from * to end, always making sure that the right sides of tr rows and wrong sides of tr rows match up. When inserting the hook through the two layers of work, the hook should always pick up 2 threads, never just one thread or a number of threads, this makes the seam look untidy.

Figure 1 shows a seam, right side facing

Figure 2 shows a seam, wrong side facing

Figure 3 shows the type of seam that we obtain when working in rounds

Figure 4 shows an 'invisible seam'. With this lacy type of pattern, it is particularly important that we only join stitches there, where they naturally join on the pattern.

Increasing on rounds

When increasing on rounds, the turning seam should be almost exactly in the centre of the 1st increase, see figure 3 in Seams.

In order to obtain a regular increase over a round find a multiple of st(s); make up the correct number of st(s), if necessary, by increasing a few st(s) on the round prior to the increasing round.

For example, if the multiple happens to be 9 on the first increasing round, the next one will be 10, 11, 12 and so on. Never increase more than one st to each increase on ordinary tr rounds. Do not increase at random, always find a suitable multiple. For a good a-line grading with treble rounds allow 5cm (2in.) for each increasing round. Depending on the yarn increase on every 4th or 5th round. The wider the grading the fewer should be the number of rounds worked in between in-increasing rounds. Again, this should be done evenly, ie increase 3 times on every 3rd round, 4 times on every 4th round, 5 times on every 5th round. Always increase proportionally.

Decreasing

Figures 1, 2, 3 and 4 show decreasing 2 stitches on plain trebles at the end of a row. The same principle applies to the beginning of a row and anywhere else we might wish to decrease.

Note The number of loops through which we draw our yarn at the end varies, of course, according to the number of stitches we wish to decrease.

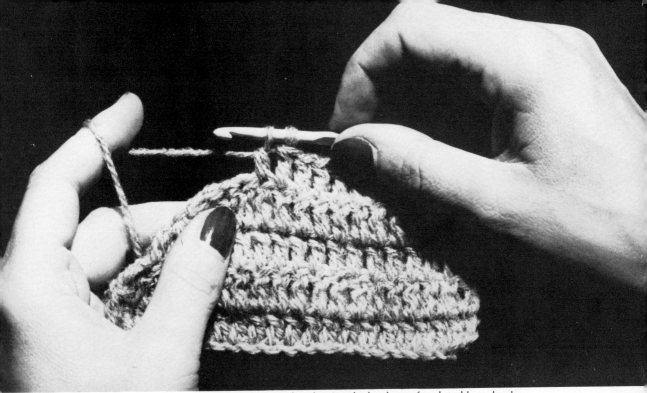

Figures 1, 2 and 3   work 1 treble into each of next 3 stitches, leaving the last loop of each treble on hook

Figure 2

Figure 3

Figure 4   yarn round hook, now draw through all 4 loops on hook

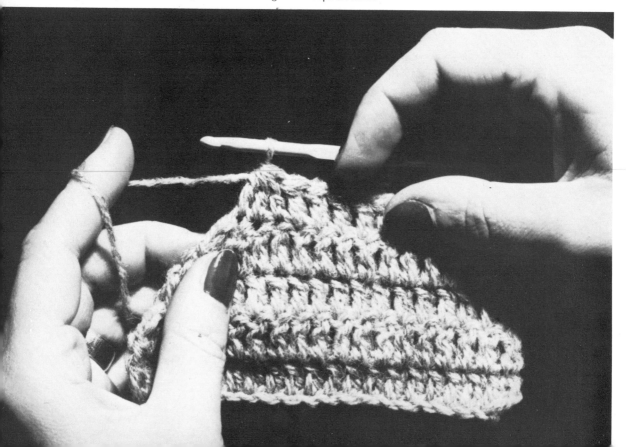

Decreasing with a lacy pattern

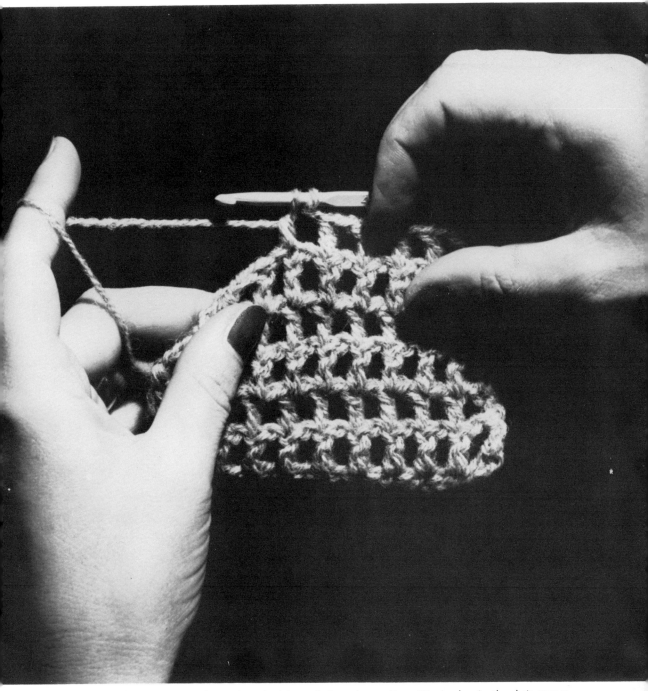

Figures 1, 2 and 3 demonstrate our decreasing principle applied to a lacy pattern. We simply miss the chain spaces in between and decrease in the usual way.

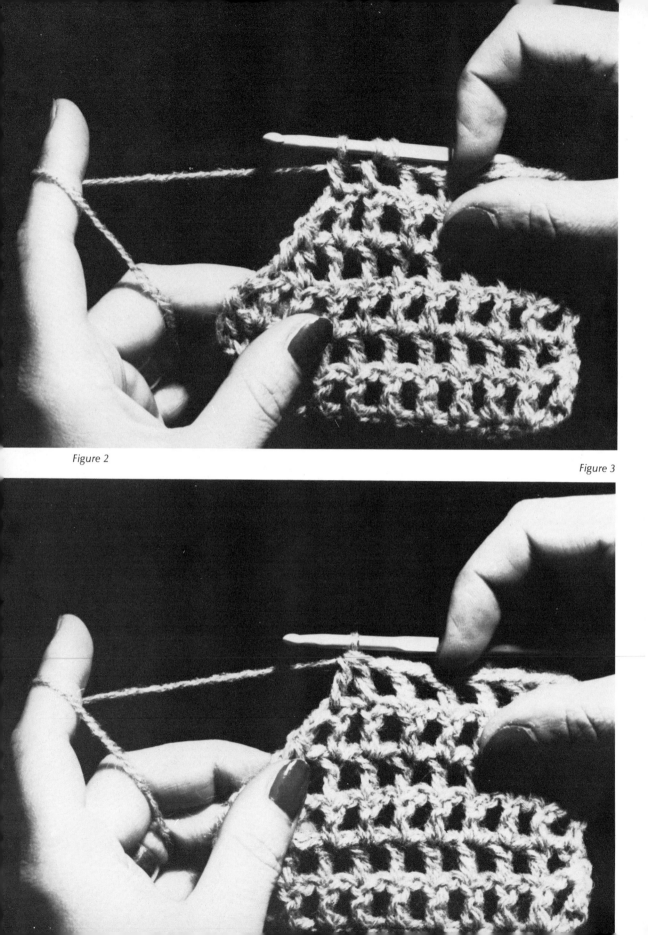

Figure 2

Figure 3

Figure 4 demonstrates the decreasing at the beginning. Instead of working stitches together, we work 2 or 3 ch (depending on how tight we wish the edge to be) and carry on with our pattern.

Reshaping

The same principle can be applied to reshaping. On the following pages I will demonstrate how to give a shawl a new look by taking off the tip.

If we then add a different lacy border to the shawl a completely new look is obtained.

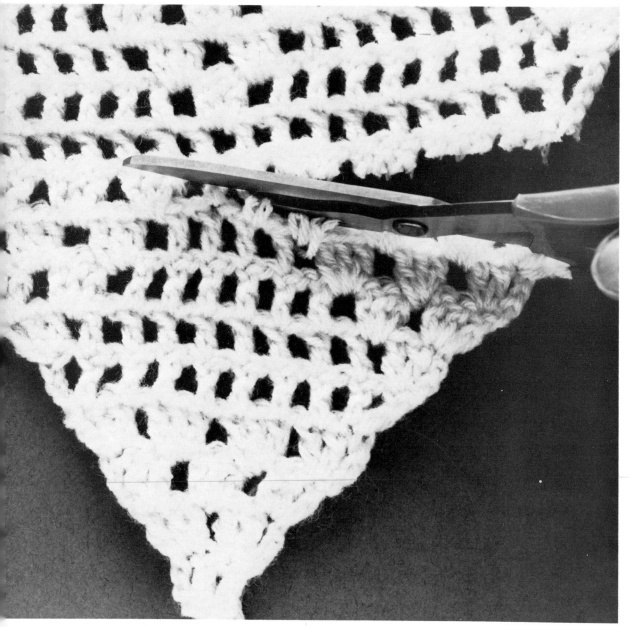

Figure 1 cut off tip through the centre of the row. Pull off loose ends gently to obtain 'open' trebles (figure 2).

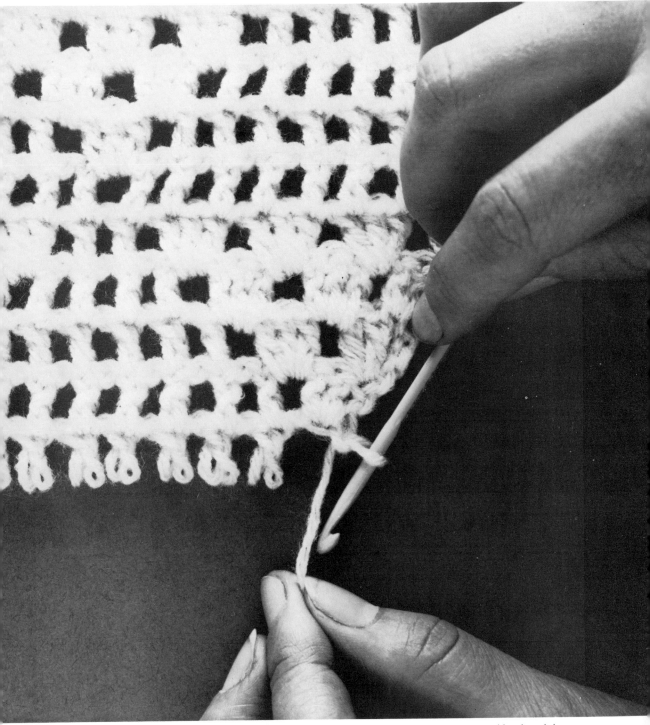

Figure 2 rejoin as shown. Work 3 ch * insert hook through the 2 loops of the 'open' tr. Yarn round hook and draw through all loops on hook; 1 ch

Figures 3, 4 and 5   repeat from ★ Figure 2 to end

Figure 4

Figure 5

Invisible mending

There can be occasions when a little knowledge on how to mend a damaged area can be quite useful. This also applies to shortening, reshaping etc.

Below I will demonstrate step by step how to 'invisibly' mend a very badly scorched area,

Figure 1

The very first rule is not to be worried about taking a pair of scissors to the garment. Luckily you cannot 'drop' stitches with crochet and any stitch that is unintentionally destroyed with the scissors can be reworked as the following pages will demonstrate.

Figure 2   cut out damaged area in a square. The vertical cuts must be in the centre of the row, while the horizontal cuts should be between the stitches

Figure 3 pull off all loose ends on the vertical edges. The upper edge should be handled very gently, so as not to uncurl the 'open' trebles. Work in the same manner for the horizontal edges, but leave ends attached. Make sure the horizontal edges are absolutely straight

Figures 4 and *5*   with wrong side of work facing rejoin yarn in stitch shown. Now work 1 treble into each of next treble to end

Figure 5

Figure 6 fasten off. Knot to the loose end. Tidy up all ends on this row

Figure 7 repeat from figure 2 to 6 until the square is filled in. Fasten off, leaving a fairly long end

Figure 8 insert hook through 1st treble of last row and through the 2 loops of the opposite 'open' treble

Figure 9 yarn round hook and pull through all loops. Continue like this to end. Tidy up ends

Figure 10   shows the mended area

uffs

There are, of course, many ways of working the cuffs. In this book I have used only two methods.

The methods shown in figures 2 and 3 I recommend to the beginner. They are easy to work and have a 'finished' look.

Figure 1 shows a cuff that is either added at the end and/or used when sleeve rows (rounds) run from the shoulder downwards or vice versa. This cuff requires a certain amount of decreasing

112

Figures 2 and *3* show cuffs which are part of the pattern rows and which run the whole length of the sleeve. In other words, the sleeve is worked sideways. In figure 2 the sleeve part is worked in 3 rows of treble and 1 row of double crochet. When we get to the cuff part we work double crochet all the time. This seems to be a very easy method indeed to obtain a shapely cuff

Figure 3 shows a sleeve worked in a pattern. When the cuff part is reached, alternately work 1 row of dc and 1 row of slip stitches. Although the sleeve is worked sideways the effect on the cuff is that of a sleeve worked from the shoulder downward. It even has great similarity to a knitted cuff

114

Drop

Most garments in this book have been designed in such a way that they have to be worked from the top downwards. This simplifies matters considerably as far as drop is concerned. You simply undo the required number of rows, should any unwanted drop occur. In some cases this might, however, mean reworking edges or borders. One or two garments (skirts mainly) should be worn back to front occasionally. This avoids a 'seating' effect occurring.

For any drop that cannot be undone see pages 102 to 111 for invisible mending.

Fringe

Take required number of strands at required length for each tassel.

1st Step (figure 1)   fold strands in half.

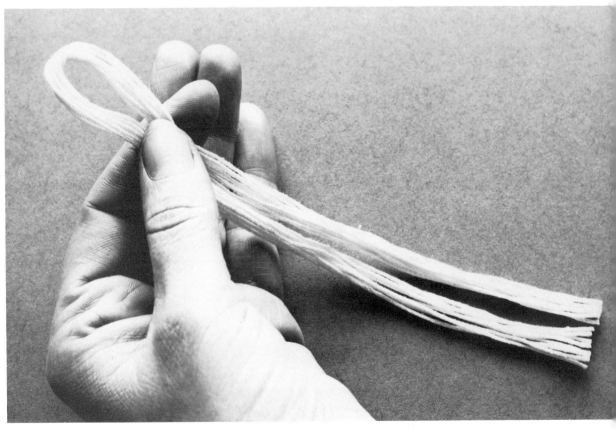

Figure 1

2nd Step (figure 2) insert hook through chain space (or loop, whichever is the case); pull looped end through chain space, winding cut ends around hook.

3rd Step draw cut ends through looped end.

116

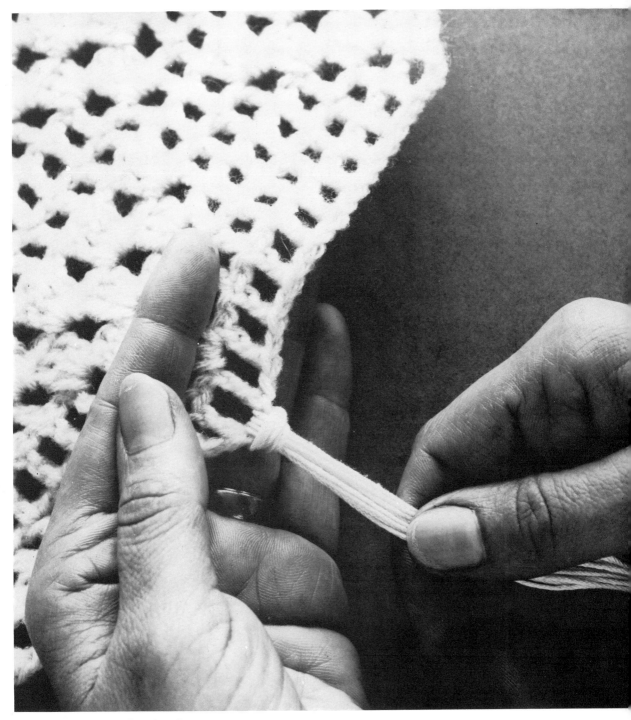

4th Step (figure 3)   pull ends tight.

Draw string

Take required number of threads at twice the
required length and twist at both ends in opposite
directions, until a good twist has been obtained.
Fold in half and allow to twist into a rope by itself.
The tighter the threads are twisted the firmer they
will twist into a rope.

Measurements

Where several alternative figures are given, the
first is to fit an 81cm (32in.) bust. Directions for the
larger sizes ie bust 86:91:96cm, 34:36:38in., are
given in brackets.